POLICY STUDIES IN EMPLOYMENT AND WELFARE NUMBER 10

General Editors: Sar A. Levitan and Garth L. Mangum

The Role
of the Private Sector
in Manpower Development

Charles A. Myers

The Johns Hopkins Press, Baltimore and London

HD
5715.2
M9
1971
c.1

This study was prepared under a contract to the Task Force from the Office of Research and Development, Manpower Administration, U.S. Department of Labor.

The Johns Hopkins Press, Baltimore, Maryland 21218
The Johns Hopkins Press Ltd., London

Library of Congress Catalog Card Number 72-152912

International Standard Book Number 0-8018-1275-5 (clothbound edition)
International Standard Book Number 0-8018-1324-7 (paperback edition)

Originally published, 1971
Paperback edition, 1971

Contents

Acknowledgments vii

Introduction 1

1. Training for Production Jobs 5

2. Formal Training Programs for Skilled Crafts and Maintenance
   Jobs 15

3. Hiring and Training the Disadvantaged 24

4. Training for Office and White-Collar Jobs 51

5. Developing Technical and Professional Manpower 61

6. Management Training and Development 71

7. Private-for-Profit Training and Vocational Schools 81

8. Summary and Conclusions 85

References 91

Acknowledgments

An earlier draft of this manuscript has benefited from comments by my colleagues on the National Manpower Policy Task Force. Professors Myron L. Joseph of Carnegie-Mellon University and Frederick H. Harbison of Princeton University were on the reading committee assigned to review the first draft, and Professors Sar A. Levitan of George Washington University and Eli Ginzberg of Columbia University also gave me many helpful comments. Dr. Howard A. Rosen, director of the Office of Research and Development, of the Manpower Administration of the U.S. Department of Labor, provided special reports on some of the research and demonstration projects funded by the Department.

It is also a pleasure to acknowledge the research assistance provided by Mr. John Lawrence French, Jr., a graduate student in the Sloan School of Management at M.I.T. He helped check the literature, made extensive notes, and read early drafts of some of the sections. My secretarial assistant, Patricia Macpherson, typed the first draft and persevered through the extensive revisions.

The Role of the Private Sector in Manpower Development

Introduction

Despite the rapid growth of employment in the governmental and other not-for-profit parts of the American economy in recent years, the private sector is still by far the largest employer and developer of manpower. Expanded federal manpower training programs, which will approach a budget of nearly $3 billion by fiscal 1971, reflect this fact in their direct and indirect expenditures for training for private sector jobs. About $422 million was budgeted for pre-employment and on-the-job training programs, largely in private industry; but many of the other programs have as their ultimate objectives the training of people for eventual employment in the private sector.

There are various estimates of the relative size of the private sector. Data for total nonfarm employment in 1969 show that the private sector accounted for 82.5 percent of the total in each year (Table 1). An earlier estimate of the "not-for-profit sector" share of total national employee compensation arrived at a percentage of 23.9 for 1963, so that by this different measure the private sector accounted for 76.1 percent in that year, down from 81 percent in 1950 (50).* A separate 1965 analysis of the service economy yielded a 73 percent figure for employment in the non-

* Numbers in parentheses refer to numbered references beginning on p. 91.

Table 1. Total Non-Farm Employment, by Sector, 1969

(*thousands*)

Sector	1969	Percent
Private	57,911	82.5
Non-private	12,288	17.5
Total	70,139	100.0

SOURCE: *Manpower Report of the President, March 1970,* Table C–2, Total Employment on Private Payrolls: Annual Averages, 1947–69.

farm private economy (which excluded services in households and institutions as well as in government-owned enterprises) (47). The private sector similarly measured contributed 76.7 percent of the 1965 GNP in constant dollars. It should be noted, however, that some private employment, particularly in firms with government contracts, is supported directly by government expenditures.

In summary, by almost any measure, the private sector has accounted for around three fourths to four fifths of the employment in the U..S non-farm economy. Cyclical variations will occur, of course, because an expanding full-employment private sector will provide more opportunities for manpower development than will a contracting one with growing unemployment.

An advanced industrial economy approaching the "post-industrial society," such as the United States, has a wide variety of skills and occupations, reflecting in part the complexity of the job hierarchy on the demand side, and in part the variety of educational preparation and pre-employment training for these job opportunities (the supply side). But most manpower development takes place *on the job* and in the sequence of movement from job to job within the organization as well as between firms, industries, and occupations. Some of this represents short-term mobility, but much more occurs over an individual's working lifetime. While there is undoubtedly some movement between sectors in the economy, the greater size of the private sector means that private employers play the major role in recruiting, training, motivating, and developing the talents of our labor force.

How well or poorly they do this is the central focus of this study. The literature of personnel administration and industrial training is full of information about this experience, but it frequently lacks research support. The objective of this monograph is to review that research and other evidence that indicates the extent to which private firms have been successful in developing manpower at most occupational levels. Some findings will be better documented than others.

In the sections which follow, we shall consider reported studies on production and maintenance workers (including the apprenticeable crafts), on special programs for "disadvantaged" workers, on white collar and office employees, on professional and technical employees, and on management and executive development programs. The role of the private-for-profit training schools and institutes will also be reviewed briefly, as reported in various studies.

It will be obvious that this list does not correspond exactly to U.S. Census occupational classifications. Several of the latter comprise the "white collar and office employees" sections: clerical and sales workers and some service workers. "Production and maintenance workers (including apprenticeable crafts)" include the Census groups of "operatives," and the "craftsmen" part of "craftsmen and foremen." In private industry, foremen are generally considered a part of management, but the management section in this report excludes individual proprietors and, of course, public officials. The professional and technical employee section corresponds exactly to the Census group. Thus, the occupational groups covered in this analysis account for about 90 percent of total employment, although perhaps 17.5 percent of the total is in non-private employment. Farmers and farm laborers are excluded, as are "laborers" as such. But some production workers start as laborers, and the discussion of the "disadvantaged" may include some in this group as well as others not in the labor force prior to employment.

At the end of each of the sections in this study, the gaps in our knowledge about training and development will be pointed out as "unanswered questions." The report will conclude with a brief summary of the findings of this research review, with some evaluation of the performance of the private sector in manpower development. There will also be some observations on the role of governing in assisting the private sector in its training and development programs.

1

Training for Production Jobs

The usual process of training and manpower development for production jobs in private firms involves informal on-the-job training and upgrading more often than formal in-company training programs. In organizations characterized by promotion-from-within policies, and especially in unionized firms where seniority considerations play an important role in upgrading and promotions, new recruits are hired for entry-level jobs, sometimes at the bottom of skill ladders. They then qualify for higher rated and more skilled jobs after they have acquired experience on previous jobs in a job family or skill ladder.

The newly hired employees usually have some minimal educational requirements, sometimes a high school degree for certain firms, jobs, and occupations. They may or may not have had to pass some type of employment test, and usually a medical examination is required. They are interviewed and screened by the personnel department and possibly by the foreman or supervisor under whom they may work. Thus, the average new employee possesses some qualifications on which training and promotion can be reasonably based, although the existence of thirty-to-sixty day "probationary periods" in union agreements and the absence of any employment guarantee elsewhere means that management can dismiss the new employee if he fails to meet performance standards within the first month or two. The presumption is that such failure indicates potential lack of promotability to higher skilled jobs. The extent to which these considerations have been modified under the programs to hire the disadvantaged will be considered in chapter 2.

Firms with relatively stable employment levels have more restrictive hiring standards, other things being equal, than those with expanding employment, and thus place more emphasis on those applicants with prior experience (12). It is probable, therefore, that the static firms do less training generally than the expanding firms. The same considerations apply across the economy or regionally when aggregate demand for the products or services in the private sector is stable, expanding, or contracting.

YOUNGER WORKERS AND ENTRY JOBS

Within a local labor market, some firms will seek new employees with previous work experience, because of the nature of their job requirements and job hierarchy. Other firms, particularly for entry-level or routine and unskilled jobs, will take new entrants without prior work experience. For example, in a study of five firms in the New York metropolitan area, differences were found in the activities of young workers prior to employment:

Workers at the utilities were strikingly alike; the incidence of military service was slightly greater at Utility A and post-high-school education and training greater at Utility B. Auto Assembly differed from others in that its workers constitute a more homogeneous group. Of the 80 workers for whom detailed information was available, only 3 had no labor market experience prior to coming to work at the company and only a few had full time post-high-school education or training. The department stores were characterized by larger groups who came directly to the company for their first job (17 and 20 per cent respectively) and by more involvement in post-high-school education and training (46).

In this study, young workers had weak occupational attachments; they had made a number of job shifts, three fourths of which involved changes in occupations. This is further corroboration of the earlier labor market studies which showed that mobility of younger workers, particularly males, is high and often complex, involving shifts in employer, industry, occupation, and location, often in several combinations (113, 123, 93). In other words, many younger workers try out different jobs and employers before they later become more or less attached to one occupation and/or employer. Occupational attachment is obviously stronger in the skilled trades, as in printing, construction, and some service industries, and for apprenticeable occupations in industry, such as tool and die makers. Employer attachment is stronger where the internal labor market is characterized by a particular configuration of jobs and technology in the firm as a consequence of its product or service. In either case, the new "attached" employee generally has the opportunity in many industries to proceed along some promotional ladder leading to higher paying, more skilled jobs. But the process of moving up this ladder is often a long one, stretching over a decade or two in firms that are not rapidly expanding.

THE INTERNAL LABOR MARKET AND TRAINING

This promotion or progression within the enterprise often involves, as Dunlop has pointed out, "a single administrative set of rules governing the movement of employees," within an internal labor market of the firm (34). The ports of entry may be at various levels in the occupational hierarchy, in addition to the lowest entry jobs: those with special training or education may enter directly at higher levels, as in maintenance jobs requiring apprenticeship or technical and managerial positions requiring prior professional education. Furthermore, in certain manufacturing industries, such as textiles and clothing, workers are often hired directly at all skill levels.

The relative importance of on-the-job training for skills on present jobs held by workers was indicated by a 1963 government survey which showed that only 30 percent in the sample had learned their current jobs through formal training programs in a "classroom context," as in schools of all kinds, full-time company training schools of at least six weeks' duration, apprenticeship programs, and training in the armed services. A much larger proportion of workers (56 percent) had learned their current job through informal on-the-job training in the work environment (152, 55). A later study by Richard Perlman in Milwaukee, covering 150 firms (mostly in manufacturing) found that only 6 had formal training programs; all of the others relied on informal on-the-job training described as "as you work training" (115).

The importance of informal on-the-job training for blue-collar workers in much of manufacturing industry is supported by the research of Peter B. Doeringer and Michael J. Piore. They surveyed twenty-three plants in twelve different manufacturing industries in their original research, and subsequently expanded their findings to include interviews with management and union officials in over seventy-five companies, most of which were medium- or large-sized firms (32). A distinction is made between several types of internal labor markets: *enterprise* (principally blue-collar in manufacturing), *craft* (building trades, longshoring, and certain services, centered around the local union), and *competitive* (such as migrant farm labor (40), street "hustlers," free-lance writers and some nonunion craftsmen). However, about 80 percent of the employed labor force works in structured internal labor markets as opposed to unstructured competitive ones.

Nature of On-the-Job Training

On-the-job training may be given to new or less-experienced employees by more-experienced workers or by the departmental supervisor. This may be by instruction and demonstration, as a part of production work, or by delegating some part of the work to the trainee who progressively learns more of the job. The process has been aptly described by Doeringer and Piore:

For blue collar manufacturing jobs, the hallmark of on-the-job training is its informality. The process is variously described as "osmosis," "exposure," "experience," or "working one's way up through promotion." Very often, on-the-job training is not recognized as a distinct process at all; it is simply assumed that a worker who has "been around" for a while will know how to do certain things. For relatively simple operating jobs, new workers are typically given a brief job demonstration. They then begin to produce on their own, receiving occasional help from foremen or neighboring operators. On more complex jobs, particularly those involving maintenance or repair, the novice may serve as an assistant to an experienced employee. In other cases, training takes place along a promotion ladder in which work on the lower level jobs develops the skills required to learn the higher level, more complex skills. Workers may also learn other jobs by observing neighboring workers without them being aware of what is going on. Sometimes even the trainee is not conscious of the learning process. Thus, even where the jobs within a department are not skill related, the ability to perform them is correlated with the length of time the worker has "been around" (32; 57).

In some cases, there are more formal aspects to on-the-job training. New production workers are first trained in a "vestibule school," usually somewhere in the plant, away from the pressures of production, but with the same machines or equipment under the guidance of an experienced worker as instructor. In the absence of similar equipment and good trainers, however, vestibule schools lack the value of direct on-the-job training.

On-the-job training involves additional training costs to the firm. For example, while an experienced worker or a supervisor is training the new workers, there is some time lost by them to production or other duties. The newly trained employee may cause some materials wastage or even machine breakdown by improper use, and his initial product may not be of high quality. These training costs may be difficult to separate from production costs, as Doeringer and Piore point out, but they are generally recognized by managers as training costs associated with production. When in tight labor markets, experienced workers cannot be hired outside for the more skilled jobs that may constitute other points of entry, less experienced workers are put on these jobs, again at some cost to production. As a consequence, however, they may gain additional skills.

Many of the skills that workers learn on the job, through employer investment in the training costs outlined above, are specific to the particular enterprise, as has been indicated earlier. In larger firms, the process of job description and analysis, combined with job evaluation, indicates a sequence of jobs in a series of job ladders, with corresponding rates of pay attached to jobs by a weighting of different factors (116). While there is some similarity in so-called "key jobs" between firms in the same industry or even in the same locality, a large number of jobs are more or less unique to the enterprise. Therefore, no prior pre-employment skill training can qualify an employee for a series of jobs in the job hierarchy of a particular firm; only on-the-job training which builds on some prior general education or experience can do this for the employee who has the motivation to learn and to qualify for more skilled jobs.

THE ALLOCATION PROCESS AND TRAINING OPPORTUNITIES

Personnel policies, custom, and rules established through collective bargaining govern the allocation process which determines the jobs for which employees may qualify by training and experience as well as into which they can be promoted. The width or narrowness of the seniority unit, the basis for transfers, and the relative importance of ability or qualifications (as determined by management) and seniority in promotions are specified in collective agreements with unions, or unilaterally by management in nonunion firms. Seniority as a factor in layoffs and recall is also part of the allocative mechanism, since the employer generally has an interest in recalling experienced employees before hiring new ones, and employees have an interest in the job security inherent in the seniority principle (32, 134).

The same allocative process, combined with further on-the-job training, operates when there are changes in existing jobs as a result of technological changes broadly defined. Present employees generally expect to be trained for the new jobs, especially if existing jobs are eliminated by the change or if the new job carries a higher rating. A survey of thirty-six companies by Industrial Relations Counselors, Inc., found that production employees "have proved to be equipped for learning the new tasks in a changed technology as a result of their skills, qualifications and experience acquired before operations were modernized." On-the-job training in these cases is described as follows:

New equipment has often been developed and "debugged" on the factory floor, contributing to the ease of training workers. In this process, line management has worked closely with the engineering force. By the time the automatic machines have become operational, supervisors have known how to run them, and in turn, have been able to teach their subordinates right on the job. Often, the employees who were eventually to operate the machinery have worked in proximity to the debugging process, and, therefore, have learned a good deal about its operation by observing the new processes during the break-in period (6).

Sometimes, however, technological changes involving blue-collar workers are so substantial that more formal retraining programs are necessary. This occurred in the well documented case of the Xerox Corporation, which decided in 1959 to curtail the production of sensitized photographic paper and to expand production of copying machines. With projected gradual curtailment of the former operations over one year, and union support, management arranged with the Rochester Institute of Technology to conduct skill training on representative machines and in assembly of machines, in addition to classroom instruction in mathematics and blueprint reading. Of two hundred eligible employees, sixty-eight finally entered the training program which lasted six weeks. A study of this experience concluded that "unskilled production workers in a manufacturing industry can be retrained, in a relatively short time, to an acceptable degree of competence for occupations that are not only new to them, but also ranked slightly higher in the skill hierarchy" (42).

This type of formal retraining program for blue-collar workers is undoubtedly found in numerous other similar situations. It is likely to have more relative success than one which involves plant closures for economic and technological reasons, with displaced employees retrained at company expense for other jobs in the local labor market or, with the prospect of geographical relocation, in newer modern company plants established in other localities (133).

SOME UNANSWERED QUESTIONS

This brief review of training programs, primarily on-the-job, which the private sector uses to develop the skills of blue-collar workers, leaves some questions unanswered and requiring further research.

1. How good *is* the informal on-the-job training? If skills are acquired by "osmosis"—by watching skilled operators—do new employees learn jobs as fast and as well as they might with really competent instruction?* During World War II, Job Instructor Training was developed to show supervisors and skilled workers how to instruct new employees effectively, but it is doubtful if these tested techniques are as widely used now. The very informality of much on-the-job training described in the studies reviewed earlier may mask some poor instruction. Furthermore, under wage-incentive systems, it is well known that experienced employees may withhold from management the shortcuts and other methods they have discovered to increase productivity, and they are also less likely to share this knowledge with new employees.

2. Is on-the-job training more effective in terms of earnings

* It will be difficult to get hard data for such an evaluation, however. The Difficulties are suggested in an unpublished study for the Office of Research and Development, Manpower Administration, U.S. Department of Labor, by Gerald G. Somers of the University of Wisconsin, "Pilot Feasibility Study of Training in Business and Industry," 1970. Only 170 of the sample of 248 firms said they had training programs, and of these "it was found that only a relatively small proportion of the firms kept records concerning training and trainees which could be readily transferred to a questionnaire form," and most of these were firms wtih over 1,000 employees.

improvement than is "institutional training" of the sort sponsored by the Manpower Development and Training Act? There have been a number of cost-benefit studies of the latter, but only one comparing the two (92). Additional efforts to measure relative costs of training, as borne by employers, and training benefits to both employers and trainees, are needed. How important is a high school education or its equivalent for promotion above the entry-level jobs?

3. Much of the research on training has involved larger firms, but what about the training practices of smaller firms? In one New England study covering large as well as small firms, two thirds of the small firms (eight-to-forty-nine employees) reported training, mostly on-the-job training (67). Possibly this was better than in the larger firms, but possibly it was worse. We don't know.

4. The specificity of much on-the-job training may limit the worker's ability to acquire broad training which would permit him to move between different types of jobs, firms, and industries. The breadth of training may be a larger issue in apprenticeship programs, discussed below; but among production workers, it is also related to the width of the seniority unit, the opportunity for transfer, the availability of trial periods on more skilled jobs, and other rules governing the allocation process. Research comparing different types of allocation systems over a period of time in particular firms or industries might shed more light on these questions, especially as between union and nonunion firms. The tendency of younger workers to shop around, as noted in a number of studies, may or may not result in broader training backgrounds than those developed by recruits who stay with one firm from the beginning of their work experience. But again, we know too little about lifetime career patterns and the acquisition of skills by blue-collar workers, as well as by other occupational groups.*

* The longitudinal studies under way at Ohio State University under the direction of Professor Herbert S. Parnes, with support from the Office of Research and Development, Manpower Administration, U.S. Department of Labor, will be helpful on this question. These examine the labor force behavior of 20,000 persons, in different age groups.

5. The acquisition of new skills by employees and employer investment in training are likely to be more effective if the *motivation* of employees and employers is high toward these objectives. To the extent that employees are not upward-mobility oriented, or employers are worried about investments in training which will benefit some other employer if the trained men leave, training opportunities are underutilized. These questions are related to the efforts which will be reviewed in a later section to provide jobs and training for the disadvantaged, and to subsidize private employers in providing this kind of training as well as training for skills in short supply.

2

Formal Training Programs for Skilled Crafts and Maintenance Jobs

The dividing line between on-the-job training for production workers and more formal programs for skilled crafts and maintenance jobs may not always be sharp. But the nature of the apprenticeship pattern for the acquistion of skills in certain occupations is basically different because of its partial formality and its emphasis on the acquisition of a broader range of skills. In the 1963 Department of Labor Survey, 40 percent of the craftsmen and kindred workers had formal training (schools and apprenticeship programs) (55).

Apprenticeship programs in the building and construction trades are the most common; but apprenticeship for the highly skilled mechanical trades in manufacturing is also of long standing. More recently, government-subsidized on-the-job training for skilled occupations in short supply preceded the NAB-JOBS program for the disadvantaged. Each will be discussed briefly in the following subsections.

APPRENTICESHIP IN THE BUILDING AND CONSTRUCTION TRADES*

About fifteen building and construction trades crafts, plus several specialities, have apprenticeship programs that are locally administered by unions and employers through joint committees all over the country. Some programs are complex: there is a standard apprenticeship for carpenters, but separate ones for the related carpentry jobs of soft-floor layers and dock builders, among others. They vary in length: for example, plumbers and electricians have four- to five-year programs; bricklayers generally three years; and some others such as lathers, roofers, and painters as little as two years (150). But the length of the program is not only related to the time it is considered necessary to learn the trade, either in related instruction or on the job. It also puts a time limit on employers using apprentices at lower-than-craftsmen wage rates.

The manpower planning mechanism which determines how many apprentices will be admitted to each program yearly is a local one and tends to be conservative, so there are often long waiting lists of applicants. But one national union, the Operating Engineers, has a national joint apprenticeship council which can review local committee's decisions and revise them upward or downward on the basis of projected national needs in the craft. Since local construction employment is more volatile, this requires that journeymen or craftsmen be ready to move between localities to follow the availability of work.

Despite this apparent formality and restrictiveness, the fact is that in no trade is apprenticeship the *only* route to entry or to journeyman status. Among plumbers in a large Northeastern city, for example, two thirds of the new members each year come from nonunion men who get local licenses, and one third from union apprentices who have completed the training program. The

* Much of this material is from a forthcoming book by my M.I.T. colleague, Professor D. Quinn Mills, *Industrial Relations and Manpower in Construction* (Cambridge, Massachusetts: M.I.T. Press, 1972). Chapters 7–9 deal with formal training programs.

equivalent proportion among electricians in this same city is about fifty-fifty. A study of construction labor supply in upstate New York found that 21.5 percent of 784 craftsmen (bricklayers, carpenters, electricians, and operating engineers) indicated that their *only* source of skill was informal on-the-job training in construction. Nearly 20 percent of the operating engineers reported that they had once been laborers or truck drivers on construction jobs (44).

However, it seems clear that union-sponsored apprenticeship programs are more common in the building and construction trades than for similar skills in manufacturing. George Strauss has concluded that this is due basically to market structure; in construction there are small firms unwilling and unable to assume the burden of training workers whose primary loyalty is to their craft rather than to a single employer (141). In contrast, large manufacturing firms have the resources and the incentive to train because they have a skill hierarchy and other means to retain loyalty to the firm through seniority and fringe benefits related to seniority.

The best programs are said to be in the mechanical trades, electricians, pipe trades (plumbers, etc.), sheet metal workers, etc., which have had expanding demand for skilled workers, and for which the tasks require greater skill and intelligence than in other trades. Apprenticeship also serves another purpose in providing breadth of training: "To a considerable extent, the function of the apprenticeship program is to train the cadre and the leadership, the core of the really skilled men who provide guidance to the others" (141).

The lower rates of pay which apprentices receive for long periods account in part for the dropouts, which averaged 50 percent in 1960 according to a Department of Labor study. Those who do complete the programs tend to remain in the craft, as indicated by a 1959 study by the Bureau of Apprenticeship and Training, which found that of 3,378 persons who completed apprenticeship programs in 1950, 93 percent were working at the trade or a related trade six years later, and more than 50 percent had advanced to supervisory positions or had become independent contractors (151). The study which cited these findings concluded:

> The relatively few who acquire journeymen status as a result of completing a formal apprenticeship training program seem to realize long-term benefits in psychological and financial security. Even apprenticeship training dropouts look kindly on their training, explaining that only financial hardship or the possibility of more immediate financial gain influenced them to drop out of the training program (42).

In addition to working on the job with a journeyman, and learning the trade in this manner, apprentices under Federally registered programs are required to attend a minimum of 144 hours of related classroom instruction off the job in vocational schools or other schools. A sample of those interviewed in seven crafts in California and upstate New York were reported to have attended such classes against their will, feeling that "classwork was impractical, irrelevant, boring, and a waste of time." The study concluded, however, that there was a need for more and better related instruction because of the increasingly technical nature of the jobs (140).

Selection of apprentices in many programs in the past has been based on the father-son or relative relationships. A 1956 study by the Bureau of Apprenticeship and Training of the U.S. Department of Labor found that of 3,278 persons who had completed apprenticeships in 1950, the following proportions were in the same trade as their fathers: construction, 32 percent; metalworking, 14 percent; mechanic and repair, 8.8 percent; and printing, 9.3 percent. Prior to recent developments, reviewed below, apprenticeship training has quantitatively been of little importance to blacks, since the total number of openings each year is small. In 1964, for example, only 54,491 new apprentices were admitted, but only a small percentage of these were Negroes (83).

18

Apprenticeship in Manufacturing and Transportation

There is apparently less formality in many apprenticeship programs for skilled mechanical trades in manufacturing. While some are joint union-management programs, as in graphic arts, others are employer-initiated to meet continuing needs for highly skilled machinists, tool and die makers, and similar skilled workers. Even so, the extent of formal apprenticeship programs is probably limited to large firms, and accounts for only a small percentage of the total trainees in manufacturing.

Apprenticeship and alternative paths to become qualified and competent tool and die makers have been explored in a study in the Boston area by Horowitz and Herrnstadt (64, 45). No important differences were found in competency (as rated by foremen of the employees interviewed) among apprenticeship training, vocational high school training, and informal on-the-job training (described as "picked-up trade"). However, the *shortest* and most effective route to competency in the trade was by a combination of vocational high school and apprenticeship; the longest were vocational high school only and "picked-up trade" only (115). In the relatively informal path of on-the-job training/ "picked-up trade," men were classified as tool and die makers before they felt competent. While less than 30 percent of those interviewed had served apprenticeships either as machinists or tool and die makers, the breadth of their training and their ability to do a variety of very complex tasks led to superior performance ratings. There was fairly unanimous agreement among all of the sample interviewed that practical work experience was the most useful part of the training, but workers expressed the need for more formal education, especially in mathematics.

Despite the breadth of training under apprenticeship programs, the authors concluded that because of machine shop specialization, job ladders, and changing technology, training programs should not all attempt to produce broadly trained craftsmen competent in a variety of tasks. Some specialized skills are needed, as are competent people who can work under the supervision of others.

While most of those interviewed were high school graduates, failure to finish high school (25 percent) and/or training programs (20 percent) did not necessarily mean inability to achieve a high degree of work competency, if there was a capacity and a desire to handle increasingly difficult assignments. On upward mobility to supervisory ranks, the study found that the proportion of managers and foremen who had been apprentices earlier was roughly equal to the percent of employees interviewed who had served apprenticeships (less than 30 percent).

There are similar findings in other industries, such as printing, and in air transportation (57). For example, new employees start as helpers in unionized commercial printing shops, and apprentices for printers (typographers) and pressmen are drawn from the helper group. Apprentice training includes both classwork and on-the-job training, lasting four years. There are few progressive ladders in the crafts, except in large shops. The craft unions collaborate with employer associations to update the training of journeymen in a technologically changing industry.

Apprenticeship in air transportation is only one of the routes to craft jobs, the other two being through private vocational schools and by on-the-job progression from semiskilled jobs. Only two major airlines were reported to have formal apprenticeship programs, consisting of classroom instruction and on-the-job training. During 1968 the airlines claimed to have spent about $125 million on training of all personnel, only 15 percent of which was for training maintenance people. Line mechanics, however, received at least forty hours of training each year to keep up to date on equipment changes.

SOME QUESTIONS

This review of apprenticeship programs suggests areas for further study:

1. To what extent are present educational and training requirements in apprenticeship programs really necessary to achieve competent journeyman status? Clearly, some all-round skilled

craftsmen are needed, but should there be shorter programs for those seeking more specialized skills?

2. The Boston Tool and Die study and some studies in the building trades indicate that men achieve journeymen or craftsmen status without apprenticeship. Is this likely to grow as skilled-crafts shortages occur? What combinations of vocational schooling, formal apprenticeship, and on-the-job training are likely to be most effective in specific crafts?

3. Formal apprenticeship programs are defended as training programs, and are criticized as restrictions on entry, especially by minority groups. To what extent have minority applicants for apprenticeship programs been able to pass entry requirements, and what has been their relative success in completing apprenticeship programs as presently constituted? Are other special programs for minorities desirable? Some of these questions will be explored further in a later section of this study.

SUBSIDIZED ON-THE-JOB TRAINING FOR LABOR
SHORTAGE OCCUPATIONS

Subsidized training in private firms and labor organizations through the U.S. Department of Labor's manpower programs, preceded the NAB-JOBS program for the disadvantaged workers. Under MDTA, a total of 382,000 workers were enrolled in these on-the-job training programs during the seven fiscal years, 1963–69. While 65 percent of the enrollees were unemployed prior to training, 53 percent had completed high school or more; 58 percent had three or more years of prior gainful employment; 68 percent were males; 69 percent were white; and 67 percent were primary wage earners (78). They were clearly not "disadvantaged," although there has been more emphasis in MDTA programs recently on the disadvantaged.

Relatively little is known about the success of these specific programs. Apparently only one study, by Taylor and Piore, has been made of this experience, and it was confined to three dis-

21

persed employment occupations facing labor shortages: tool and die makers, offset printers, and restaurant cooks and chefs (145). With subsidies from MDTA funds, these programs were sponsored by multi-establishment organizations, employer associations in the tool and die makers and cooks-chefs programs, and an employer association in cooperation with a trade union local for the offset printers. The argument for subsidy rested in part on the fact that in these dispersed employment occupations, each employer is small in relation to the market, and ordinarily might lack incentive to train his own skilled workers when he might expect to hire them in the market.

The printing and tool and die programs were similar in many respects to the on-the-job training programs discussed in chapter 1. However, the offset-printing training was basically a vestibule program designed for training journeymen letterpress operators in the new skill of offset printing for which there was a claimed shortage in the industry. Most trainees were recruited directly by the union, and attended in many cases without their employer's knowledge. Only ten of the twenty-nine trainees used their training with any regularity. The tool and die program, organized by a private training group, included an initial ten-week vestibule program with classroom instruction in math, physics, and tool management, followed by on-the-job training in the process of production.

The restaurant training program for cooks and chefs was also initiated by a private training organization which saw the need for trained cooks and chefs. It helped form a restaurant association, and got government support for a training program which started with a ten-week period of full-time class instruction, followed by forty weeks of training on the job together with evening classroom instruction. A trainer-coach helped place the trainee, and participating restaurants were paid a stipend per trainee to cover the chef's time in teaching on the job. While the program was well designed, it proved difficult to evaluate its effectiveness relative to the alternative method called "employee-programmed," in which those who sought training as cooks and chefs were motivated to learn these skills themselves by frequently changing jobs in order to work under different master cooks and chefs.

Would these programs have been developed without government subsidy? The study was not able to give a definitive answer to this question, because a comparable control group in each case was not available. But the authors conclude that much of the training that was subsidized may well have been in the interest of the employer to finance himself. But this tentative conclusion also raises another: Can it be expected that employers in these industries or others always act fully in their own economic self-interest? Furthermore, in these dispersed employment industries characterized by many small employers, can it be assumed that one will invest in training that may benefit a competitor if the trained man leaves? The existence of these external diseconomies has been the rationale for subsidized on-the-job training in labor shortage cases.

3

Hiring and Training the Disadvantaged

In the preceding chapter, we have noted the limited experience with subsidized on-the-job training under MDTA. For the most part, these training slots were filled with the better qualified among the "disadvantaged" applicants, or were designed to meet specified skilled shortages. One study of OJT subsidies to small employers in New Haven, Connecticut, indicated that the largest single group (twenty-two out of ninety-five) viewed the subsidies as payments for which they did nothing in return. Thirty-nine were disheartened by the behavior of trainees and either refused to use the OJT program again or put new conditions on continuing its use (52).

Similar attitudes among Cleveland employers were found by Iacobelli (65, 66). He interviewed without prior appointment a stratified sample of 151 Cleveland area employers, most of whom favored government subsidies for training disadvantaged labor. But most also felt available subsidies were not enough to cover costs, and they were also reluctant to train the disadvantaged for fear of decreasing the pool of potential promotable employees. Many felt that private industry should handle skill training and leave remedial education and psychological problems to government programs. Only 25 percent of the firms, mainly large ones, participated in government manpower programs.

The failure of the OJT part of MDTA to involve private industry in hiring the disadvantaged led manpower planners in the Department of Labor to consider other approaches to stimulate more private commitment (98). This began with a series of Manpower Administration contracts, which helped launch the National Alliance of Businessmen's Job Opportunities in the Business Sector (JOBS) program. Eligibility for these programs was rather broadly defined.* The intention was to help those with labor-market disadvantages, sometimes also called "hard core" unemployed.

Some of the disadvantaged are those who have held other jobs, but lost them, or who lack the qualifications to get and hold a job in the primary labor market. Their employment may have been irregular, but they have the motivation to seek steady jobs with a chance for advancement. Many of these are black ghetto residents, but not exclusively. On the other hand, many of those characterized as "hard core" are young black single males who may never have held a job in the primary labor market, but get income from a variety of irregular employments and activities (some illicit) in the ghetto itself, or the secondary labor market, in Michael J. Piore's phrase (117; 74). Their motivation, attendance, and other habits often distinguish them from other employment applicants, and lead to problems of adjustment into the work force in the main private sector. Some part of what Dean Morse calls "the peripheral worker" may also be in this group. He defines peripheral workers as those who have work experience of any kind other than full time for a full year, and these numbered about 38 million of the 86 million in the labor force in 1965. These workers are "overwhelmingly concentrated" in agriculture, services, and retail trade. Many are low skilled, nearly half are

---

* The MA–3 eligibility criteria were: "Poor persons who do not have suitable employment and who are either: (1) school dropouts; (2) under 22 years of age; (3) 45 years of age or over; (4) handicapped; or (5) subject to special obstacles to employment." U.S. Department of Labor, Manpower Administration, *Request for Proposal MA–3*, 1968. Item 5 refers primarily to discrimination or other difficulties faced by minority groups, principally blacks.

women, many are young and non-white. While high personal cost and serious underutilization characterize much of this group, peripheral work may also be beneficial to those who cannot work full time throughout the year (91).

PRE-NAB EXPERIENCE WITH HIRING THE DISADVANTAGED

Prior to the recent national drive spearheaded by the National Alliance of Businessmen (NAB) in cooperation with the U.S. Department of Labor, there were numerous examples in private industry of firms making special efforts to employ the disadvantaged. Some of these developed in response to labor shortages, leaving black applicants as the primary source of new labor supply. In part at least, this appears to have been true of the automobile and other basic industries, although even here special efforts were made by firms to recruit, educate and train the disadvantaged*.

Lockheed Aircraft appears to have made a notable effort to develop special remedial education and skill training in specific jobs for disadvantaged unemployed workers in its Georgia and California plants. Turnover in the Georgia plant for those who completed the program compared favorably with normal plant

* See Arthur W. Saltzman, "Manpower Planning in Private Industry," in Arnold R. Weber *et al.*, *Public-Private Manpower Policies* (Madison, Wisconsin: Industrial Relations Research Association Series, 1969), p. 90, for some information on the Ford Motor Company experience with an Inner-City hiring program initiated in 1967. For a number of other basic industries, see Herbert R. Northrup *et al.*, *Negro Employment in Basic Industry—A Study of Racial Policies in Six Industries,* vol. 1 (Philadelphia: Industrial Research Unit, Wharton School of Finance and Commerce, University of Pennsylvania, 1970). Industries covered were automobiles, aerospace, steel, rubber tires, petroleum, and chemicals. In each of these, blacks were predominantly in unskilled and semiskilled blue-collar jobs, although in some, the small percentages in the craftsmen and clerical jobs was increasing slightly under outside pressures. For a review of the initial studies, see Vernon M. Briggs, Jr., "The Negro in American Industry: A Review of Seven Studies," *Journal of Human Resources,* vol. 5, no. 3 (Summer 1970), pp. 370–81. A number of other industries, manufacturing and nonmanufacturing, have been studied in the Racial Policies in American Industry Report Series by the Wharton School group, under Professor Northrup's general direction.

turnover, and quality and quantity of work in the California plant was roughly equal to those of other new employees (62).

In some cities, special organizations were developed by the private sector to stimulate recruitment and training of the disadvantaged. Among these were the JOBS-NOW programs in Cleveland and Chicago (16), the Work Opportunities Unlimited (WOU) in St. Louis, and Jobs Clearing House in Boston (119). Subsequently, the formation of the Urban Coalition in a number of cities led to further efforts to induce private firms to provide employment for the disadvantaged, part of a broad attack on urban problems (39).

Reasons Why Business Did More

In addition to finding new sources of labor in the face of labor shortages, other external factors or pressures led private firms to hire and train more of the disadvantaged. Undoubtedly, there has been a growing social commitment to urban problems on the part of the top management of a number of large firms. However, in pointing to this "continually expanding social responsibility" (at least prior to the business downturn of 1969-70), Levitan, Mangum, and Taggart point out:

It is trite but true that businesses operate for profits, and business resources cannot be committed on a large scale without the promise of profits. Cursory analysis has shown that most of the achievements so far have been by firms seriously threatened by ghetto problems, those which are insulated from the costs of social commitment, or those which stand to benefit from such activities. Despite the rhetoric, traditional rules of the game have changed little (73).

Social commitment was undoubtedly sharpened by the black riots in such cities as Detroit, Chicago, New York, Boston in 1966 and 1967. Also important were pressures from other sources, including the federal government's Plans for Progress and Equal Employment Opportunity Commission, similar state groups, and community agencies such as the Urban League, NAACP, CORE, and antipoverty groups. Subsequently, the National Alliance of Businessmen brought business pressure to bear on a large number of firms (118).

These external pressures have led to internal organizational changes which help to explain relative success in hiring more disadvantaged applicants. They have been analyzed in a study of twenty Chicago area firms and organizations, six of which were classified as relatively successful, and fourteen as relatively unsuccessful (54, 68). Among the important internal structural factors were profitability ("profitable companies are more likely to engage in training"), manpower needs, higher wage levels, higher skill requirements, less rigid recruitment and screening policies, and a harmonious organizational climate and union-management relations. On the degree of commitment, the following conclusions emerged:

> The degree of employer commitment is positively associated with successful performance. . . . The greater the number of individuals involved in the participation decision, the greater the commitment. . . . The more the locus of decisions is at a functionally important position in the organization, the greater the degree of commitment. . . . Conflict in attitudes and behavior during the process of the decision to participate—either within the employer organization, or between the employer organization and the community or government agencies—can reduce the degree of commitment (54).

The more successful programs also had full-time administrators, and their perceptions of trainees were a predictor of program performance. Furthermore, their access to persons of top authority with the power to make speedy decisions was also important to success, as was the introduction of the trainee to the organization and the identification of the social and production skills needed by the trainee for his first job. Programs were more likely to fail when reliance was placed on on-the-job experience alone, but too much time in the classroom before job training was just as bad. As earlier successful programs demonstrated, this study also concluded: "The best combination appears to be classroom training interspersed with controlled on-the-job experience, then entry on the job." But, "Even if the transition [to work] is successful, the trainee does make extra demands on the supervisor's time" (54). The possibility of conflict exists over supervisory inattention to the trainee, or pressure for production, or the feeling by other employees that the trainee is getting breaks they don't get.

The problem has often been reported, but seldom studied carefully. The effect of supervisory treatment was noted in two studies of public utilities in a midwestern city (125). In the second study, twenty-two out of forty-nine inner-city blacks hired by one of the utilities were interviewed, and three fifths of them indicated the importance of the way they were treated by management, especially the foreman. "Considerable bolstering by management was essential to emotional comfort on the job." Also, "social aspects of the job may be particularly important to the hard core because they have been accustomed to look for their satisfactions more in human relations than in occupational success."

OTHER CASE STUDIES

Some of these same factors were analyzed in more detail in a series of case studies of successful experience in hiring the disadvantaged, many of them supported by contracts with the Manpower Administration of the Department of Labor (30, 96). Western Electric has a successful feeder plant in Newark, New Jersey, in which the disadvantaged are trained for later transfer to regular production plants. IBM established a plant in the Bedford-Stuyvesant section of Brooklyn in 1968—one of the few successful ghetto plants established recently by large business firms to provide jobs for residents (4). Both of these companies had no federal funding, but Westinghouse's four weeks' vestibule training program, which led to on-the-job training in production plants, was funded under a Department of Labor MA–3 contract (30, 120).

The Equitable Life Assurance Society began in 1962 a series of programs which attempted to provide white-collar jobs with promotional opportunities for high school dropouts. There was more emphasis on basic education in the later programs. Promotional ladders were also utilized in the upgrading program developed jointly by the Steelworkers' Union and ten basic steel companies, with federal funding. The General Electric Company was the spearhead of the Woodland Job Training Center, a cooperative training arrangement between the Cleveland Board of Education and other participating employers. Basic education, vocational training, and on-the-job training for ghetto residents led to transfer to regular production facilities. The program had both private and public financing, as did the Workers' Defense League Apprenticeship Training Program, discussed below.

A more recent evaluation of the experiences of Boeing, Eastman Kodak, Westinghouse, United Airlines, and Bankers Trust Company concludes, as did the earlier studies, that skill training is not enough. [.Support systems are required to help change the expectation of failure and low esteem which many "hard core" have of themselves in regular employment. In addition to remedial education and job skill development, most of these firms have some form of "sensitivity training" for supervisors, assignment of counselors to trainees to help them with work adjustment and personal/home problems, and follow-up procedures to reinforce the idea that the trainee has the chance to perform a useful job and to spot the need for further training.] But it was considered important that the support system terminate at an agreed upon time, and that the foremen should be included during training and support as much as possible (94).

How Much Has Been Done?

Quantitatively, it is difficult to determine how important these efforts to hire more disadvantaged workers have been. Within the particular firms, progress has certainly been made, as the case studies indicate. But in the aggregate in a particular urban labor market, the evidence is mixed, as a review of the Boston labor market has shown:

> It is possible to argue from the data that blacks have made sub-stantial gains relative to whites in the percentage of the more desirable jobs which they hold in the Boston labor market. A review of practice and policy in individual companies can support this view. Most of the large or nationally prominent employers have instituted special programs to hire and train black or other minority workers; there is increased sensitivity in all of these companies to the special problems faced by blacks in their establishments. . . .
> On the other hand, it is also clear that much of the progress that was achieved in the sixties was the result of adjustment to a tight labor market (31).

Is the conclusion that all of this would have occurred in a tight labor market, without any of the other pressures which led top management in many firms to commit time and money to these efforts? This would seem to be an unwarranted judgment, since it assumes that *nothing else has to happen* except a labor shortage. Reality is more complex than one-dimensional causation. What-ever the pressures and commitments, the facts seem to indicate a relative improvement in the employment and income of Negro male family heads, who, while they may not be "hard core" un-employed, certainly constitute an important part of those with labor market disadvantages during and prior to the decade of the 1960's.*

Herbert R. Northrup in his study of the aerospace industry notes that Negro participation rates have been low because of the high skill requirements in the industry. Nevertheless, there was

---

* A special report of the Census Bureau shows that Negro married men got 28 percent of the new craftsmen and operative openings that went to family men between 1960 and 1969. Since Negroes represent only 11 per-cent of the total population, this was held by Sar A. Levitan to represent "very real changes [that] are not just isolated in any particular geographical area or in any specific industry." The median income of married Negro blue-collar workers rose over the same period by 44 percent while that for white married men in the same occupations rose 27 percent (103).

an increase of Negro employment in the industry from 2.8 percent in 1963 to 4.8 percent in 1966, resulting in part from tight labor markets, increased emphasis on aircraft production as opposed to space-related activities, and government pressures against claimed discrimination. Northrup concluded: "the author has not found any company of the twenty-one surveyed which was not making a real effort to expand Negro employment" (111).

THE NAB-JOBS PROGRAM

Some of the same doubts and observations have been applied to the Job Opportunities in the Business Sector (JOBS) program launched by President Johnson in January 1968, and supported by promotional efforts by a newly formed National Alliance of Businessmen headed initially by Henry Ford II. The announced goal in fifty major cities was 100,000 jobs for the disadvantaged by June 30, 1969, and 500,000 by June 30, 1971. The program was a logical outgrowth of earlier efforts by the Department of Labor in 1967 to induce companies in five cities to bid on contracts to "hire first and train later." These MA–2 contracts were signed with only eighteen firms, so a larger effort was then launched with NAB-JOBS (73).

"The business response surprised all but the most optimistic. Forty percent of those contacted, primarily major firms, pledged to hire disadvantaged workers" (73). Within six months, 165,000 jobs were pledged for the first year, and 338,000 by July 1, 1969, for the 1971 goal. However, two thirds of these pledges were "voluntary" (later known as "freebies"), and one third involved contracts with the Department of Labor to provide hiring and training subsidies, averaging initially around $3,300 per disadvantaged employee (but more recently about $2,200). The assumption had been that hiring the disadvantaged occasioned the additional costs (mentioned earlier in the preceding section) which were beyond the employer's normal hiring and training expenses for new employees.

Pledges were secured by a staff, which at its peak consisted of

906 people, of which 871 were loaned by the business sector to the effort. Each city had a "metro chairman." The number of cities involved in the program eventually was reported to be 131, and the June 1971 target was raised to 614,000. NAB officially claimed in its first annual report that the June 30, 1969, goal of 100,000 hired was met a month ahead of schedule, and that "it is the overwhelming consensus of our Metro Chairmen in the 131 cities" that we are also on target for our June 30, 1970 goal of 338,000 disadvantaged men and women hired, trained, or in training" (95).* As of June 30, 1969, NAB reported that 1,044 training contracts had been written with companies participating in the subsidy program, and $270 million had been made available for 91,600 training opportunities. The newer more flexible MA–5 contracts totaling over $31 million covered 12,900 jobs by October 17, 1969. All of this information, as reported, preceded the slack economy which later curtailed new hiring in many firms and industries. Furthermore, hard data to substantiate NAB's claims were often not available.

Comparative Retention Rates

Reporting did not indicate at that time how many of those hired were still on the job at some later time. Subsequently, it was stated that through January 1970, of 380,000 hired, 200,000 were still on the job (78). While this is only a 52 percent retention rate over a year and a half, "in evaluating the NAB-JOBS retention rate, the typically high turnover in low-skilled entry-level jobs must be kept in mind. Only 55 percent of the labor force works full time all year, and many of these undoubtedly change jobs in the process" (73).

* Subsequently, Chairman Kendall of the NAB and Secretary of Labor Shultz in November 1969 announced the "JOBS '70" program nationwide, including small employers. In November 1970, Byron Nichols, President of NAB, reported that hires fell 80,000 short of the 338,000 target for June 30, 1970, and predicted the shortfall would be close to 150,000 below the 614,000 target for June 30, 1971.

In evaluating the JOBS program sometime in 1969, Levitan, Mangum, and Taggart concluded:

After all the available data and studies have been examined, and after national, regional and local interviews have produced conflicting information, it must be admitted that the basic questions remain unanswered. Many employers have undoubtedly made significant contributions to the welfare of disadvantaged workers and their families, but no one can say how much difference the program has made (73).

The Controversy over Data

The difficulties in arriving at generally accepted quantitative data on the degree to which the JOBS program has achieved its goals were illustrated by the May 1970 exchange between the Staff Director of the Senate Subcommittee on Employment, Manpower, and Poverty, and the Assistant Secretary for Manpower in the Department of Labor.* The former's May 1970 statement was highly critical of the JOBS program, citing statistics showing only 99,846 jobs pledged (apparently in the contract group) in almost two years, despite the Labor Department's announcement of 140,000 training opportunities for fiscal 1970 alone. An "astonishing termination rate" of 50,225 of the 84,703 hired in the two years was pointed out as one of the three reasons for the failure of the program. The other two were an underestimation of the program's vulnerability to recession, and "a serious underestimation of the resistance of businessmen to signing JOBS contracts."

* "Remarks by William R. Bechtel," May 13, 1970 (mimeographed), which followed the report of Senator Gaylord Nelson's Subcommittee, *The JOBS Program (Job Opportunities in the Business Sector) Background Information* (Washington, D.C.: U.S. Government Printing Office, May 1970). The answer by the then Assistant Secretary Arnold R. Weber was a Department of Labor news release, 11–200, "Labor Department 'Sets Record Straight' on JOBS' Program" (mimeographed), May 3, 1970. Earlier, the then Secretary of Labor George P. Shultz had testified at length on the JOBS program before the Nelson Subcommittee on May 11, 1970, but Mr. Bechtel's May 13 statement made no mention of Shultz' testimony or the data therein.

Citing some twenty-seven cases of malpractice or fraud in JOBS contracts and saying "there are many, many more examples," the Staff Director concluded:

In summary, the nationwide failure of the JOBS program to deliver jobs, education and training to the disadvantaged is thoroughly proven by the nationwide figures. The bad contracts which have been exposed are not isolated examples, but are an inevitable result of the weaknesses in the program as a whole (122).

This evaluation, which presented no comparisons with the relative success (or failure) of other manpower programs, was answered by the Assistant Secretary of Labor for Manpower in a long statement, with statistical tables. He pointed to a number of pages from the Subcommittee *Report* in which statements were taken out of context, or were erroneous. He also stated that real or alleged fraud was found in only 1 percent of the number of contracts executed since the start of the program in 1968. But more relevant for our purposes here were two sets of data in his statement: (1) a follow-up study of the income earned by former JOBS employees, using data from the Social Security Administration; and (2) a comparison of the characteristics of the employees in the contract program compared with the non-contract ("freebie") program.

Two Reported Studies

The first study was a random sample of 12,000 JOBS trainees, including those in both programs. The mean earnings of this group for 1966 were $1,499 per person, and in 1968 these same employees averaged $2,592—an increase of 73 percent, or substantially more than normal wage increases alone over the two years. "In addition, the number of employees with no reported earnings in 1966 decreased by 90 percent in 1968, and, in the same period, the number of employees with earnings between $4,000 and $6,000 increased by more than 50 percent." Assistant Secretary Weber concluded: "It is evident that JOBS employees

35

have substantially benefited from their participation in the program. This is substantiation of the viability of the JOBS program and there is no 'softness' in these statistics"(157).

The second study reported by Weber showed a remarkable similarity in the characteristics of JOBS trainees in the contract program (where presumably data are better) with those reported by the non-contract firms. Table 2 indicates the principal per-

Table 2. Characteristics of Persons Hired Through JOBS Program, Cumulative through February 28, 1970

(percentages)

Characteristic	Non-Contract	Contract
Males	74	70
Were on public assistance	15	17
Under 22	50	47
Family size 4 or less	71	70
Family income		
$0–$1,000	24	22
$1,001–$2,000	24	28
Average	$2496	$2367
Years of education		
8 or under	12	15
9–11	46	52
Weeks employed, 1969		
15–26	17	22
27–52	33	37
Negro	70	77
Spanish surname	9	12

SOURCE: Adapted and summarized from Weber, "Labor Department 'Sets Record Straight,'" appendix Table I. Data prepared by the Office of Manpower Management Data Systems, Manpower Administration, U.S. Department of Labor. The total hired in both programs 169,161 was based on the number of hiring cards received from employers and subsequently recorded.

centage comparisons between the two groups: apparently both had been hiring people with labor market disadvantage by almost any measure—age, family income, years of education, weeks unemployed, and race. There may be some question about the absolute numbers, especially since not all of the non-contract companies reported, and there was no verification of the data they did report. But it does seem unlikely that all of the non-contract figures could have been "fabricated" to match the more verfiable contract figures so closely.

Some Evaluations

The Subcommittee Staff *Report* of April 1970 contained a number of solicited letters from individual companies and some consortia (one with the United Auto Workers); these were uniformly favorable to the NAB-JOBS program (147, 30). As Secretary Shultz pointed out in his testimony to the Subcommittee:

> A reading of the letters from employers which form the bulk of your staff report provide eloquent testimony of these wider considerations. A recurring theme is the judgment that the JOBS program has induced these firms to revise their personnel practices and to discover a new source of manpower which they had formerly rejected or ignored—the poor and the disadvantaged (147).

After pointing to the adverse effects of the 1969–70 business recession on new hires under the JOBS program, the Subcommittee's Staff Report contained two observations in its summary:

> Whatever problems may be present in the NAB-JOBS program as it now stands, however, there is no question that it has made significant contributions to the problem of finding jobs for the hard-core unemployed. As with any new program, particularly one with such an ambitious goal, it is hardly surprising that problems have been encountered in attempting to carry out, on a practical and nationwide scale, one of the first programs to significantly link together Government and private enterprise for the solution of a most pressing social problem.

The benefits of the JOBS program go beyond the jobs given to thousands of disadvantaged persons. Many of the executives who have worked for NAB have gone back to their parent companies with a greatly increased understanding of the problems of the disadvantaged, and an increased concern for contributing to the solution of these problems. Firms which previously would not have thought of hiring the hard-core, or perhaps even any member of a minority group, have found that a change in this policy is a benefit not only to the hard-core disadvantaged, but to themselves.

The conclusions of the preceding discussion are generally favorable to the NAB-JOBS effort,* despite the fact that its success was associated with growing labor shortages and some of its recent problems with growing unemployment. As a consequence of the latter, the program emphasis on the contract side shifted to upgrading, although this is still largely an untested program. The change in emphasis is illustrated by the cancellation of the JOBS contract for new hires by the Chrysler Corporation, and the signing of a new contract for upgrading four hundred working disadvantaged persons on its payrolls for higher level jobs in the company. This is under a special provision in the MA–5 contracts, in which a contract firm may negotiate an additional contract for upgrading up to 30 percent of employees hired under earlier contracts.

* I am familiar with an intensive study of NAB-JOBS contracts firms in the Boston area, done by Professor Francis M. McLaughlin of Boston College. McLaughlin found that nearly every MA–3 contractor had made changes in hiring requirements, recruiting methods, testing, orientation procedures, training, supervision, disciplinary rules, and supervisory training, as a consequence of the contracts. Approximately half made use of outside training consultants. Even those who normally hired among the disadvantaged were led by the contracts to employ even more disadvantaged.

While the numbers involved were small in comparison with the numbers of disadvantaged seeking employment, the JOBS program in Boston involved sixty-one contracts as of July 31, 1970, providing 1,972 training slots. Some 1,901 had been hired by that date, and the retention rate as a percent of hires was 46. By contract type, the retention rates for MA–4 were 51 per cent on July 31, 1970 and for MA–5 and JOBS 70 (MA–6) 69 percent. McLaughlin's comparison with reported data for all U.S. NAB–JOBS contracts was 39 percent (U.S. 3/31/70) and 48 percent for Boston on April 4, 1970.

The emphasis on upgrading and promotion ladders stems from the possibility that many of those hired under the JOBS program may find themselves in dead-end or unskilled jobs exposed to lay-offs from a decline in employment or as a result of technological change. This was one of the conclusions of a study done of the JOBS program in ten SMSA's in 1970. Despite this characterization and some other negative findings, the study concluded that "there seems to be a consensus among most company personnel that attitudes among supervisory and management personnel have changed in favor of hiring more persons from disadvantaged backgrounds," and that "perhaps the most significant impact of the JOBS program upon manpower organizations is that it has reinforced the notion that the disadvantaged, if not the hard-core unemployed, can be reached, recruited, counseled, trained and employed with a great deal of success when adequate resources are marshalled and applied. Experience with the JOBS program has reinforced other findings that providing comprehensive supportive services in manpower programs for the disadvantaged is both feasible and necessary" (144).

While the study concluded, as noted, that "in most SMSA's the jobs offered were low-level dead-end jobs," this generalization does not seem to be supported by a careful reading of the full text of the report made to the Manpower Administration. For example, in Atlanta, jobs as auto mechanics, loom fixers, auto body repairmen, packagers, and arc welders were made available "in substantial numbers." Jobs for sheet metal workers, laborers, skilled machinists, and clerical jobs were filled in Baltimore, all of which experienced chronic labor shortages. In Dayton, jobs filled included machine trades, clerical and sales, structural work; and in Detroit, production machine operators, arc welders, auto assembly, draftsmen, and micro welders. Houston jobs included carpenters, shipmates, heavy and light truck drivers, moving and storing materials, and building maintenance. Disadvantaged workers in Miami found jobs as truck drivers, in stenography, and in materials moving and storing. Phoenix jobs included clerical jobs and electronics assemblers. San Diego offered auto and engineering equipment repairing, assembly and repair of electronics components and accessories, and transportation equipment assembling and related work. To call these all low-level dead-end jobs is to characterize most production jobs in manufacturing and clerical jobs in offices this way, which is a curious interpretation. Only the Jersey City jobs as a whole fitted this characterization.

Some Unanswered Questions

Presumably the better information systems claimed to be under way will provide more reliable data on the experience under the contract part as well as in the larger non-contract part of the NAB-JOBS program. Further research and evaluation based on this information may help answer the following questions:

1. What kinds of entry jobs do the "disadvantaged" get? To what extent are they dead-end? How often are upgrading and promotion opportunities provided?

2. What is the retention rate of those hired with as well as without federal subsidy, at intervals of three months from initial hiring? How does this compare with the retention rates of other new hires by contract and non-contract firms?

3. What are the reasons trainees leave before training is completed, and what are the reasons they leave within the first six months on their first job? One recent study suggests that the costs of getting and staying on regular employment are very high for young disadvantaged males, and the benefits from these jobs are not seen as substantial enough to offset the costs, which explains the lower motivation to work and the higher turnover (132). What would other studies show, and how different are the results from an analysis of the reasons for leaving first jobs given by young workers generally?

4. Individual case studies have emphasized the supportive services given trainees along with basic education, on-the-job training, more lenient initial enforcement of plant rules, more patient handling by supervisors, etc. Will further evaluation of the contract

part of the NAB-JOBS program substantiate this kind of effort, or will the critics who point to evidence of little training or supportive services (and even some fraud) be proven right?

5. Does the average contract cost per trainee result in more training and more supportive services than in the non-contract or unsubsidized firms? One study of ninety-three NAB firms with and without funding through MA contracts concluded that "the training costs are generally higher when the government is involved" (118). Eighty percent of the "company funded" (non-contract) programs cost under $2,000 per trainee, while 73 percent of the "government funded" programs averaged $2,000 and over per trainee. What would other careful studies show about costs, and beyond that, about the qualitative differences in the programs?

6. If there are serious questions about the present form of the NAB-JOBS program, what are the alternatives? Would fully subsidized public service employment be a less expensive and more helpful alternative (97)? Is the new Public Service Careers Program likely to reach more disadvantaged, be run better, and be less costly than NAB-JOBS in the private sector?*

7. The impact of the business recession on new hiring of the disadvantaged has been pointed out, although this has affected some industries (such as automobiles) more than others (such as the computer industry, for example). But is there a more general feeling by private business that it has overreached itself in hiring the disadvantaged and in dealing with urban problems generally? Will the pressures which led to the NAB-JOBS effort

* A program designed to train 151 disadvantaged persons to pass exams to fill Civil Service vacancies in municipal services and for other jobs was announced by the mayor of Boston, in a contract with the Department of Labor in July 1970. The average cost per trainee was just under $3,000, and the work on the contract itself took over a year to develop. *Boston Herald Traveler*, July 4, 1970, p. 7. By way of comparison, the average contract cost per trainee in the private sector had dropped to $2,400 by fiscal 1970, while the unit cost of the "New Careers" program was $4,200, and MDTA institutional $2,000 with no guarantee of a job after training) (157). Outright subsidy of training *and* wages for public sector jobs is a different matter, much more costly per person and as yet untested.

41

and other similar local programs lessen and business commitment decline (21, 22)? Or will private management be forced to continue to adjust itself to the kind of work force which it may have to utilize for the next several decades?

8. To what extent has the recent NAB-JOBS experience resulted in changes in recruitment, testing, placement, and other personnel policies which will have positive benefits for future employment of disadvantaged persons? There is some evidence from recent studies that this has occurred in a number of firms, but further continuing research is needed.

9. What criteria can be designed to measure the extra costs of hiring and training the "disadvantaged" to permit adequate but not excessive reimbursement through contracts (subsidies)?

THE CONSTRUCTION INDUSTRY AND MINORITY EMPLOYMENT

Despite the limited number of apprentices taken in each year in the construction industry (about 41,000 in 1965), there have been charges that many programs have effectively excluded members of minority groups, particularly blacks, and that the industry itself has relatively few blacks in skilled trades. While there were increases between 1950 and 1960, Marshall and Briggs found that blacks represented the following percentages of total apprentices in four construction crafts in 1960; bricklayers and masons, 10.75; carpenters, 1.83; electricians, .90; and plumbers and pipefitters, .71 (83). As we have noted earlier, however, apprenticeship is not the only route to employment in the industry, and later 1964 data indicate that the percentages of Negroes employed in construction have risen. For example, of workers who worked in each of the four quarters in 1964 in construction, Negroes represented 11.5 percent of the total employed by general contractors, 12.1 percent by heavy contractors, and 7.8 percent by special trade contractors (87). By 1967, the percentage of Negroes employed in selected building trades were: bricklayers, 13.6; carpenters, 6.1; cement finishers, 37.7; electricians, 3.6; painters, 9.9; plumbers and pipefitters, 3.2; excavating, grading, and road machinery operators, 6.9; roofers, 15.3; structural metal workers, 3.9; tinsmiths, coppersmiths, and sheet metal workers, 1.9; and construction laborers, 26.9 (187). While the heavy concentrations were in the "trowel trades," roofers, and laborers, Mills has noted that "by 1968, of some 410,000 nonwhites employed on an annual average in the building trades (including laborers), more than half were in the skilled trades (87).

While the average laborers' union scale plus fringes was $4.47 in 1968, the bricklayer (with 13.6 percent Negro) earned $6.31 per hour, among the highest rates. While these and other craft jobs are relatively high-paying, the additional employment opportunities for blacks are not as high as the critics sometimes imply. Mills has pointed out that exclusive of laborers and helpers, 205,000 nonwhite males were employed in the building trades crafts, and if the black employment distribution were similar to that of white males, "an additional 72,000 blacks would be employed in these trades. This figure is less than two percent of Negro male employment in 1968" in all occupations (87).

As the review above indicates, the percentages of Negro employment in skilled trades such as electrician, plumber, and pipefitter, and sheet metal worker continue to be low, even though there is some evidence of progress over past practices in these fields. Discrimination persists, especially at the local level, despite efforts by national union leaders to combat it. This is consistent with the judgment of Bok and Dunlop: "Racial prejudice is much more prevalent among the rank and file than among union leaders, and this has been true since the days of the National Labor Union in the 1860's and the Knights of Labor in the 1880's" (9; 83).

The major efforts to improve the opportunities for blacks and other nonwhites in the construction industry have evolved from pressures of the civil rights movement and resultant legislation, union efforts, training programs by other groups, and plans developed in a number of cities (partly as a result of government pressure). Some of these have been reported in the public press, but there have been only a few research studies of this experience.

Apprenticeship Outreach and Training Program

The Building and Construction Trades Council of the AFL-CIO sponsored "outreach programs" in thirteen cities which brought 620 minority youth into apprenticeship training up to October 1968, with financial support for the training from the Department of Labor's Apprenticeship Outreach and Training Program. This program also financed Outreach and training activities by the Workers Defense League (as noted below) and by the Urban League (160).

Subsequently, the Department of Labor expanded this Outreach program to sixty-three cities, covering 5,400 Negro youth for apprenticeship programs, and announced that it would extend it to eighty cities for 1,000 more young Negro apprentices (101). Earlier in 1970, the Department signed an agreement with the United Association of Plumbers and Pipefitters to place 500 blacks in line for high-paying journeymen jobs in areas where there is a labor shortage. Under the agreement, the national union and thirty-three major construction companies are to recruit and train minority members who are beyond apprenticeship age and may lack schooling although they are working in the trade. The Department of Labor allocated $1.4 million to pay for the on-the-job training and supplementary classroom instruction (100). The New York local of this union was considered arbitrary in excluding Negro applicants for its apprenticeship program (83). In 1969, the International Union of Operating Engineers developed a pre-apprenticeship training program, with Labor Department funds, for young blacks who would later enter the regular apprenticeship program for excavating equipment operators (60). Similar agreements have been negotiated with the Laborers, Plasterers and Cement Masons, and Carpenters international unions. However, there is no published research indicating the extent to which any of these programs have been successful in bringing large numbers of blacks into journeymen status.

The Workers Defense League: A Successful Program

The activities of the Workers Defense League in recruiting and tutoring young blacks in New York City to take apprenticeship tests in construction craft unions have been examined in some detail by Marshall and Briggs (82, 83). Originally a human rights organization, the WDL moved into the apprenticeship area in 1963. It had participated with other groups in an effort in 1963 to get 25 percent of all publicly aided construction in New York City for Negroes and Puerto Ricans. This resulted in the appointment of a biracial committee to screen and interview 1,624 nonwhites who considered themselves qualified for apprenticeship or journeymen status in the construction industry. The committee concluded after extensive work: "We had been led to believe that there were thousands who couldn't gain admittance into the building trades unions. As a committee we felt that the numbers who came forward were small and those qualified were even smaller in number" (82).

This experience evidently persuaded the WDL to recruit and tutor minority apprentices, and this first required the development of a booklet describing all apprenticeship programs in the city, to acquaint qualified applicants with requirements, and to encourage others to acquire the necessary qualifications. With initial foundation grants, and subsequent support from the U.S. Department of Labor, the WDL has actively sought out interested minority applicants, building up good relations with many of the local unions along the way. Its first training or tutorial program to prepare Negroes and Puerto Ricans for apprenticeship exams started with a court-ordered open examination for sixty-five apprenticeship positions in Local 28 of the Sheet Metal Workers Union. Only one WDL-prepared man qualified eventually, but in subsequent apprentice classes in the same local union, the WDL achieved much higher qualification rates: 12 of 25 placed in the top 30 taking the exam in 1965, 25 among the 65 selected in 1966, and 18 of 60 in 1967. "Thus, in two and one-half years the WDL

45

placed fifty-one Negroes in Local 28, or 20 percent of all apprentices admitted" (82). Similar efforts were made to gain minority admittance in other unions, with particular difficulty in the Plumbers Local 1. By November 1967, however, 245 young men had been placed in apprenticeship through WDL activities, and only 6 percent had later dropped out.

The WDL program was later expanded to fourteen other cities, with financial support from the Department of Labor. By December 1969, 1,700 had been placed (800 in New York City) with less than an 18 percent dropout rate. As noted earlier, there are similar programs in other cities under the sponsorship of the Urban League and local building trades councils. According to Marshall and Briggs, the WDL program developed in New York City is the prototype of the others. "The WDL-type operation is therefore designed to do whatever is required to get Negroes into apprentice programs and set in motion the forces which will expose the fundamental defects in existing procedures and clear the way for fundamental remedies" (82; 30, 27).

City-Wide Programs to Increase Minority Employment in Construction

Civil rights and minority groups have protested what they considered to be discrimination against nonwhites on construction jobs financed by the federal government, on construction under urban renewal and the Model Cities program, as well as in construction generally. Perhaps the most publicized result has been the Philadelphia Plan initiated by the Secretary of Labor in September 1969. This established "targets" for minority employment on federally financed construction in the city, but according to one account, it "has not begun to produce even minimal gains toward its modest goal of breaking the color barrier in six construction trades. As a result, the Department of Labor is moving to sue a number of contractors" (105).

Partly under the threat of government pressure of the Philadelphia type, eighteen other cities developed plans locally to increase the employment of minorities in construction. These included Boston, Denver, and St. Louis, among others. For example, the Boston Plan embraces all phases of the construction industry and was developed jointly by local union, construction, and minority group leaders. Through a nonprofit corporation to implement the program, some 2,000 minority group members will be recruited and trained for employment in skilled building crafts in the Boston area over the next five years. In lauding this Plan, Secretary of Labor Hodgson earlier also warned some 73 other cities that they must develop their own plans to employ more blacks in 1970 or face government-imposed racial hiring targets or quotas.*

This type of minority employment involves special problems not present in the apprenticeship programs discussed earlier. As Mills has pointed out, many residents of central city areas in which urban renewal or Model Cities construction is proceeding "do not possess the necessary skills to be employed at the journeymen rate, and often these persons are ineligible for apprenticeship by virtue of age, academic background, or other qualifications" (87). Consequently, the "home grown" city plans such as Boston's have begun to establish programs with formal on-the-job training and related instruction, at intermediate wage rates starting at the apprentice rate and rising by a step scale every six months until the journeyman's rate is reached. The experience with these programs deserves continued study.

Some Unanswered Questions

This brief review of minority employment in the construction industry raises some policy questions, on which further research is needed:

1. Are present apprenticeship requirements in skilled craft

---

* A number of recommendations were made to the Secretary by the National Manpower Advisory Committee on steps to be taken to increase the employment of Negro journeymen and apprentices in the construction industry (78).

unions discriminatory, and if so, how should they be changed? If they do discriminate against unqualified applicants, how should existing qualifications be lowered, if at all? High school education or its equivalent is one requirement, as evidence of ability to use numbers is usually related. Is the discrimination the result of poor schooling for blacks, rather than "discriminatory" qualifications for apprenticeship? Are apprenticeship tests "culture free"?

2. Does successful apprenticeship require high motivation and commitment, as some writers have suggested? If so, does this explain why it has been difficult to recruit the more disadvantaged young minority group members for these programs, and to retain them once they begin (87)?

3. To what extent would more effective enforcement of antidiscrimination legislation further increase the employment of blacks in the construction industry?* Is a target or quota approach effective in increasing black employment?

4. Apprenticeship is not the only route of entry to skilled construction trades. To what extent are blacks more successful through informal routes, including the city-wide plans mentioned earlier?

5. In vew of the criticism by civil rights leaders and some academic scholars of the record of the construction industry in

* "Legal sanctions have not been especially successful in getting Negroes into apprenticeship programs, though they have perhaps had the effect of creating a climate among apprenticeship sponsors which is conducive to change. . . . Legal actions have had differential effects on the establishment. As noted earlier, to the extent that government antidiscrimination programs have been based on misunderstandings of the nature of apprenticeship and its importance to the sponsors, it has strengthened the defensiveness of the apprenticeship establishment, and has generated suspicions about the motives of government and civil rights officials in controlling the apprenticeship system, ignoring qualifications, imposing quotas, and requiring preferential treatment. At the same time, however, antidiscrimination programs have succeeded in breaking down some of the barriers and strengthening those persons within the apprenticeship establishment who favor equal apprenticeship opportunities." Marshall and Briggs, *Equal Apprenticeship Opportunities* (Ann Arbor: A joint publication with the National Manpower Policy Task Force, November, 1968), p. 23.

employing minorities, what is the evidence that its performance in this respect is poorer than the record of industry generally in employing blacks in high-paying skilled jobs?

6. Is there evidence of more minority employment in the non-union sectors of the construction industry, particularly in home-building (59)?

OTHER PRIVATE NON-COMPANY PROGRAMS

The work of the Urban League in the Apprenticeship Outreach and Training Programs has been mentioned earlier. The league also provides other training programs for blacks interested in qualifying for skilled jobs in a variety of industries. Since November 1964, the Urban League is reported to have placed in jobs and trained more than 45,000 people, most of them disadvantaged blacks. During 1970 the League received one of the largest MDTA-OJT contracts ever awarded by the Department of Labor —a two-year $9.1 million contract to train 9,000 disadvantaged people in thirty cities. Private employers are said to regard highly the League's placement efforts.

Another private nonprofit organization is the Opportunities Industrialization Center, founded by a black Philadelphia minister, Rev. Leon H. Sullivan, in 1964. Its earliest supporters were private firms such as General Electric, Bell Telephone of Pennsylvania, Western Union, Westinghouse, and I.B.M. The O.I.C. program has two parts: (a) a feeder program which is prevocational, focusing on changing attitudes and remedial education; and (b) skills centers which provide training in such areas as drafting, sheet metal work, machine shop, chemical laboratory technician, power machine operating, electronics assembly, etc.

By January 1969, 1,500 were enrolled in the Philadelphia program and 20,000 nationally in 71 O.I.C. programs which were established in other cities with support from private employers. In 1969, about $2 million was raised from private employers, but government funds from Labor and other departments provided $18 million. Rev. Sullivan emphasizes, however, that all O.I.C.

programs start initially with private help, since placement depends primarily on the private sector. He claims that 90 percent of O.I.C. trainees get "good-paying, skilled jobs," and after six months 80 percent are still working on the jobs for which they are trained (143).

Impressive as these claims are, there has been only one independent study of O.I.C., which raises some questions about eventual job placement data. For example, of 1,389 "job placements" claimed in 1966, power sewing was the largest, followed by OJT (presumably with private employers); feeder programs which provided training in communications and computational skills, personal grooming, etc., run by O.I.C. itself, and then "job applicant" (again presumably in private industry). IBM took 99 trainees; electronics assembly, 96; secretarial work, 79; and office practice, 66. Much of the training was developed in conjunction with prospective employers, and apparently there were large percentages of women enrollees in many programs (142).

4

Training for Office and White-Collar Jobs

In the previous sections, on-the-job methods of training were emphasized for most blue-collar jobs, especially in production and maintenance, and for the disadvantaged. Formal training is used to remedy educational and other deficiencies for the disadvantaged, and formal apprenticeship programs are an important route to the skilled trades in construction. However, for many white-collar jobs, formal training is often a prerequisite for employment, even though there is subsequent on-the-job training. This section will review evidence from reports and research on office and other white-collar jobs in the clerical, sales, and service occupational groups.

In the 1963 government survey of formal training background of workers between twenty-two and sixty-four with less than three years of college, the following percentages reported learning the job by various methods:*

* Adapted from table on p. 18, *Formal Occupational Training of Adult Workers,* Manpower Administration, Office of Manpower, Automation and Training, Manpower/Automation Research Monograph No. 2, December 1964. Since one-third of all respondents indicated more than one way, the sums of the percentages exceed 100. "Formal training" includes training obtained in schools of all kinds (including company training schools lasting at least six full-time weeks), apprenticeship, and the Armed Forces. "Casual" includes learning from a relative or friend, or "just picked up" and other similar methods.

	Formal	*On-job*	*Casual*
Clerical and kindred workers	53.6	71.4	29.5
Sales workers	23.4	60.2	47.4
Service workers (except private household)	24.6	45.5	42.7
All occupational groups (total of 11)	30.2	56.2	45.4

It is clear that the highest relative formal training is among the clerical and kindred workers. The figure of 30.2 percent for formal training for all occupations is the result of higher-than-average percentages for professional, technical, and kindred workers (64.6), and craftsmen, foremen, and kindred workers (40.6), offsetting the low percentages for operatives and kindred workers (12.9) and laborers (6.9).

CLERICAL AND STENOGRAPHIC JOBS

Many of these jobs are held by females, most of whom complete some form of commercial or business education before they find employment. "For clerical occupations . . . high schools were the chief training medium for all but telephone and office machine operators. For these two, the respective major sources of training were company training schools and special schools" (152). It should be noted, however, that clerical and stenographic workers with a high school education still require some further training on the job. Employers, therefore, make additional investments in on-the-job training to develop the special skills and methods required by their particular needs, as the table at the outset of this section indicates. A different conclusion, however, was reached by Richard Perlman in his study in Milwaukee. He reported that only 5 percent of office jobs were filled by workers who had required additional company training. "This widespread acceptance of prior office training indicates that the individual requirements for office jobs do not differ significantly among companies, so that the school instruction usually requires little modification for application to specific jobs" (115).

What type of formal training has been most helpful for clerical jobs? One survey of secondary schools as preparation for youth employment in Pennsylvania noted: "Graduates of the vocational curriculum obtained more manufacturing jobs while graduates of the academic and general curriculum obtained more white collar, primarily clerical jobs." However, there were only "a limited number of vocational offerings available to females. Office occupations accounted for about half of all the students, male and female, enrolled in the vocational curriculum. It was the only vocational program open to girls which could accommodate any significant number" (70). Secretaries and stenographers are also trained in post-secondary courses in business schools or in junior colleges, of varying length depending on the skills taught. Some are also four-year college graduates, often with specialized additional training (155).

Another route to all white-collar jobs, which has been reported in only one study, is advancement within the firm from blue-collar jobs. This study by Johnson and Stern was confined to men hired or promoted to white-collar jobs during the prior two-year period, with special attention to those who had at least one year in a blue-collar job during the preceding five-year period. Twenty-two percent of the total sample were in the prior blue-collar group. The largest portion of these (39 percent) had moved into managerial jobs (primarily foremen), followed professional and technical jobs (24 percent), clerical (21 percent), and sales (17 percent). About 30 percent had some prior full-time higher education, but had dropped out for various reasons to take blue-collar jobs. A majority had enrolled in part-time schooling after they began work, so they were not typical blue-collar workers. The study found that "a majority of the *interemployer* moves were made *prior* to the blue- to white-collar shift, while *intraemployer* moves predominated for the blue- to white-collar shift for subsequent job changes. . . . For most men in the sample, shifts from blue- to white-collar jobs took place within the same employer organization" (69). The initiative generally came from the employee himself, and for some the shift initially involved a financial sacrifice for expected long-run advantages of white-collar employment. The study recommended that "employers should give consideration to adoption of formal programs for upgrading blue-collar workers into professional-technical and clerical-sales classifications, as they now identify and train blue-collar workers for manager-supervisor jobs" (69).

There are a few reported studies of training disadvantaged and minority groups for office and clerical jobs. In the Northrup study of the aerospace industry, Negroes accounted in 1966 for 2.8 percent of all office and clerical workers. The difficulty of upgrading Negro clerical employees was linked to lack of prior training as well as to locational housing problems. Northrup reported (111):

> Aerospace industry officials—and most others—would often prefer to train high school graduates initially, rather than have to retrain them. The girl who thinks that she has learned stenography often resents being retaught and feels discriminated against because she is unaware how lacking in skills she actually is.

A somewhat different experience is reported in the Procter & Gamble Company, where small groups of Negro women, mostly recent high school graduates and single "were given special training in order that they might be better prepared for secretarial and clerical positions in the main offices and technical centers of the firm." All but two of the forty-three women who began the training completed it and "most of these were offered, and accepted, regular office positions" (89). Four content areas were emphasized in the formal sixty-hour training program: spelling, grammar, vocabulary, and arithmetic.

OTHER WHITE-COLLAR JOBS

Some clerical and stenographic jobs are found in almost every industry, but there are also other types of white-collar jobs in banking, insurance, hotels and motels, wholesale and retail trade, and many service industries. Available studies refer to some specific jobs in most of these industries.

1. *Bank tellers* represent about 20 percent of the nonsupervisory work force in banking, and they are usually high school graduates who have passed math and verbal aptitude tests given by the employer. In larger banks, training begins at a teller training center for as much as two weeks at full pay, often using self-instructional programed material, and role-playing with colleagues and supervisors in learning to count money and striking proof. After this formal training, "the trainee rotates through several training branches, working closely beside a coach, for three months, before he is actually assigned to a window of his own" (57). This example illustrates the importance of company formal and on-the-job training, *following* the formal secondary school training and aptitude requirements prior to employment.

Another study of hiring standards in a number of jobs in New York City and St. Louis included the bank teller. Prior education (usually academic high school) was considered important by 78 percent of the (unspecified) sample of banks interviewed in New York City and 100 percent in St. Louis. They reported that an inexperienced worker could be trained on-the-job in 7.2 weeks in New York and 11 weeks in St. Louis, and an experienced worker in 2.8 and 2.4 weeks in each city, respectively (28). All of the banks reported that an attempt was made to determine the worker's aptitude, his interest and/or temperament, and his personality; and all considered his appearance important.

For other banking jobs, banks also provide in-company as well as outside training opportunities. One survey reports that 89 percent of all banks have tuition refund plans and in 1966 banks spent some $31 million on education and training, mostly for tuition reimbursement. The American Institute of Banking has more than 100,000 bank employees attending classes, study groups or participating in correspondence classes. It holds formal classes in three hundred cities, and offers twenty-nine banking, bank related and communications courses to all levels of bank employees (57).

Banks, as well as insurance companies, have participated in the effort to provide employment and training opportunities for the disadvantaged applicants, as mentioned in an earlier section. One bank example is that of Chase Manhattan Bank in New York, which began a JOB program late in 1967 (19; 24). At present, JOB trainees get four weeks of full-time study (mathematics, business fundamentals, reading, and other language skills) and then spend five months working and studying on alternate weeks. By the end of 1969, 128 of the 255 workers who finished the six-month program were still with the bank—a retention rate of 50 percent. Presumably, many of those who left used their training to find other related employment. The program was revised in mid-1969 to relate the academic material constantly to the prospective job inside the bank, rather than the earlier formal instruction in black and Spanish culture, trips to museums, exhibits, etc. The trainees themselves told Chase that "this cultural stuff was a waste of time"; instead they wanted to know about the bank.

2. *Insurance* company jobs are primarily clerical, below the level of agent and supervisory positions. Companies normally have remedial courses for new employees who need additional work in math, spelling, and typing. High school graduates are preferred, and initial skill training for clerical positions is done on the job under the direction of the first-line supervisor. Most upgrading is also done on the job, but one survey reported that for seven higher clerical positions such as correspondence clerk, fifteen to thirty hours of formal classroom training are often given (57). Insurance agents and brokers have generally had prior college training, in business subjects (including insurance) or in liberal arts. After being hired, they receive further formal training at insurance company home offices or in agencies. Some is the formal classroom type of training; some is training on the job. Many take additional courses or seminars at colleges and universities and seminars sponsored by insurance organizations (155).

3. *Telephone* traffic department workers are primarily operators, with the remainder in positions of service assistant and service observer. Long-distance operators are generally given three

weeks of training; others a few days. Information people need almost a week of on-the-job training, but in New York City a pilot training program has been developed to upgrade the quality of directory assistance by training information operators for six to seven weeks at a cost of $700 per person (57).

4. *Hotels and motels* require desk clerks, reservations clerks, and other special white-collar people. Most training is apparently informal and on the job, although graduates of hotel school curricula in higher education get some prior formal training. A recent collective bargaining agreement between the New York City Hotel Association and the Hotel Trades Council provided for the "training of employees for promotion and advancement." Each hotel contributes $1 per month per employee to a Hotel Industry Training Fund, with occupations and training methods to be decided by a joint labor-management council. The study reporting this development indicated that no actual training had yet been done (57).

The hiring standards study included "hotel clerk," and indicated that in New York City, high school or some high school work was the minimum level of education by 48 percent of the firms; and in St. Louis the figure was 82 percent. As in the bank teller's job, an attempt was made by all firms before hiring to determine the worker's interest and/or temperament, his personality, and appearance. An experienced worker could be trained to the particular firm's requirements in about two weeks; but an inexperienced worker required more than twice that number of weeks (28).

The other white-collar jobs covered in the hiring standards study were perhaps less skilled than those reviewed above. The *cashier-checker* in retail trade required less formal education, but academic high school was preferred. Less training time was specified: about one week for experienced workers, and twice that in New York City as compared with nearly seven times that in St. Louis. Appearance was considered very important, but interest and/or temperament, and personality less so. High school or some high school was preferred for *salespersons (parts),* but on-the-job training times were longer than for cashier-checkers—twenty to twenty-seven weeks in New York and eight and a half to thirty-three weeks in St. Louis for experienced and inexperienced workers, respectively. Clearly, this is an example where training is required for working familiarity with the firm's parts inventory. Aptitudes, interest and/or temperament, personality, and appearance were all rated highly in prospective applicants. To a lesser extent, the same factors were important in the shipping and receiving clerk job (28).

A somewhat contrasting review of education and training requirements reports that "manufacturer's salesmen" are generally college graduates, especially those selling technical products and equipment. Those with little or no training beyond high school generally sell nontechnical products. Beginning salesmen also usually have some formal company-sponsored training before they start on the job, including job rotation as well as some formal classroom training. Retail salespeople, on the other hand, receive primarily on-the-job training, and some may come from high schools with distributive education programs (155).

Jobs Created by the New Technology

A number of jobs have been created by computers, which require keypunch operators, programers, console operators, and systems designers, among others. In the insurance industry, an early user of computers, one study reports that "keypunch operators are trained from scratch and usually spend two or three hours a day in a classroom for an average of forty hours. Console operators and programmers are trained on-the-job but get supportive training in classrooms conducted by both the company's training department and equipment manufacturers" (57). Training programs run by IBM, Honeywell, and other computer manufacturers are available in many cities. Systems designers usually have a background in higher education, particularly in mathematics, but get additional formal training either in computer manufacturing firms or other computer applications.

58

One report mentions training unskilled people for data processing jobs. An MDTA-financed program in Washington, D. C., by the Institute of Computer Technology (a private, nonprofit firm) began with a ten-week phase for all trainees which provided familiarization with EDP concepts and jargon, followed by a twenty-week program for the best students in training for computer programmer technicians. Others were put in a different twenty-week track to study the operation of unit record equipment. In the first program in 1964, thirty-two out of thirty-four graduates were placed; the second program in 1966 had thirty-three still in training at the time of the report (33). Twenty-eight of these were men; twenty-four were high school graduates and seventeen had some college. Their background was mostly clerical, but a few had prior sales experience.

A similar case is also reported in the Washington, D.C. area, where a training program was begun by the Sequential Computer Corporation under an NAB-JOBS contract with the Department of Labor. Two groups of 60 young Negro women were hired to become "data typists." After a one-week orientation program, they were organized into 12-person teams with experienced workers as members. Each team's production was measured against the others, so that intra-team cooperativeness in training was stimulated. By the end of 1969, 80 of the 120 were still employed by the firm at $2.65 an hour; turnover and absenteeism were attributed to the lack of day care centers (127).

A study of electronic data processing in New York City concluded that keypunch operators required little training on the job but faced largely dead-end jobs (161). Computer operators were often retrained from tabulator operators through on-the-job training. But programmers and systems analysts were found to be in acutely short supply, with mounting unfilled openings. The shortage has resulted in some job redesign, to permit less-skilled elements of the programming task to be assigned to junior programmers or "coders." A college education with "a liberal dose of mathematics and statistics" is preferred in programmer applicants who can then be trained further on the job, or more likely, in manufacturers' schools if the firm uses that equipment. Some programmer trainees were re-treads—middle-aged people with prior experience in bookkeeping and similar jobs.

SOME UNANSWERED QUESTIONS

The preceding review indicates that comparatively little research has been done on hiring standards and training and development of workers for office and white-collar jobs. Many of the studies available are primarily descriptive. The following research questions are suggested:

1. In beginning clerical and office jobs, how important is prior formal education? Is a high school degree a screening device, or does it represent a level of accomplishment which is necessary for the subsequent training and development of the employee on the job?

2. How much on-the-job training is necessary for specific clerical, office, and white-collar jobs. Are these jobs becoming increasingly specialized to the firm, or are skills developed on the job readily transferrable to other employers so that there is little incentive for an employer to invest further in the employee's training?

3. To what extent are female, as well as male, blue-collar workers taking the initiative to qualify for white-collar jobs within the firm and in other firms? Are employers beginning to develop formal training and upgrading opportunities for this type of promotion?

4. Do most data processing jobs increasingly require specific educational and/or experience backgrounds? Can unskilled people be trained for any but the beginning data processing jobs such as keypunch operator or data typist, with limited upgrading possibilities?

5

Developing Technical and Professional Manpower

The professional and technical group includes the most rapidly increasing occupations. About 7.5 million were employed in this occupational group in 1960; by 1969 there were 10.8 million, or an increase of 44 percent in less than two decades. The projection to 1975 is for another 20 percent increase, or 45 percent since 1960—the highest of any occupational group (78). While the supply is increasing, the probability is that demand for these skills will increase even more over the next decade, with the prospect of continuing shortages. Looking to the decade of the 1970's, John T. Dunlop has observed: "I would suggest that craft shortages (technical and professional manpower) are likely to be the distinctive manpower problems of the next ten years (35)." These are the high-talent people whose training, motivation, and development are crucial to the success of many organizations.

A recent review of the technician and graduate engineer demand/supply picture projects a shortage in the supply of technicians of 160,000 to 220,000 by 1975, and 110,000 to 150,000 for engineers by the same date (124). Upgrading is suggested as the way in which firms will have to meet the technician shortage, and occupational transfers to meet the engineer shortage. Projections and predictions are, of course, subject to error; these were made before the recent cutbacks in the defense and space programs, which forced many engineers and technicians out of employment.

A more fundamental question may be raised about projections of scientific and technical manpower. Most projections involve assumptions about the continuation of past trends, which may or may not be valid. Predictions of shortages suggest a manpower crisis, but past shortages have been "resolved by upgrading sub-professionals, by utilizing personnel with peripheral skills, by restructuring programs so as to minimize shortages, by increasing wages and by numerous other methods" (149).

PATTERNS OF EMPLOYMENT AND TRAINING

Private industry is by far the largest employer of technicians, engineers, and scientists as a group. More than 70 percent were employed by private industry in 1966; government employed almost 16 percent, and education and other non-profit organizations the balance of nearly 14 percent. Government funding, of course, supported directly and indirectly much of the private and nonprofit employment of scientific and technical manpower. In private industry, engineers accounted for nearly half of the total group, technicians for about two fifths and scientists for one tenth (124). The discussion below will concentrate primarily on the first two: technicians and engineers.

Technicians

Approximately three fourths of all engineering and science technicians were employed in the private sector in 1966. The largest industries in order of technician employment were: electrical equipment, engineering and architectural services, machinery, chemicals, construction, aircraft, and fabricated metals. These same industries are among those projected for the largest percentage increase in employment requirements for technicians from 1966 to 1980 (25). The BLS 1980 projection is estimated to represent an increase of 50 percent over the 1966 total, subject to the reservations noted above.

The educational and training paths taken by technicians in private industry are varied. The latest data for the entire group are for 1965, and in that year the sources of training of 72,000 new technicians employed were as follows (with percentages of the total): upgrading (33 percent); post-secondary school pre-employment training programs (27 percent); industry training (20 percent); college and university training (10 percent); MDTA programs (8 percent); and Armed Forces training (2 percent). "Training undertaken after high school but prior to employment, however, provides the technicians that generally are in greatest demand, according to information gathered by BLS representatives in interviews with officials of companies employing large numbers of technicians" (25).

Technicians are also employed by private industry and private hospitals in health fields. Greenfield has reviewed the whole field of health manpower, some of which is employed in the public sector, and his data show that in 1965, of 2,416,000 people employed in professional and subprofessional health service occupations, nearly half (1,171,000) had three years of college or less prior training, and 525,000 more were listed as having "short training" (a term not defined in Greenfield's study) (56). Examples of occupations in the 50 percent group were diploma nurses (almost half), dental hygenists, medical record librarians, X-ray technologists, certified laboratory assistants, cytotechnologists, dental assistants, dental laboratory technicians, inhalation therapists, and practical nurses. The point of entry for most of these technician jobs was high school graduation, and the route of entry was through an approved training program, now tending to become more formal. According to Greenfield, "hospitals are probably the most important institutions in health service training," because training in them is practical or clinical and students provide hospitals with low-wage workers.*

Junior or community college training is also especially important, and MDTA programs trained 40,714 up to June 1966—primarily nurse's aides and licensed practical nurses.

Several brief research reports describe technician training programs in private industry. For example, IBM developed a retraining program for upgrading plant production people to computer electronic technicians responsible for the final testing of computers manufactured in the plant. Two courses were developed, one for trainees above average in educational background (three-fourths were high school graduates), and a second for workers in the 25th percentile of plant population. There was a lower acceptance rate in the latter group, a higher drop out rate, more time was required to complete the course and at a higher cost per trainee. It was found that while many employees previously not considered eligible could be retrained for a relatively high-level technician job, their educational background, particularly in mathematics and technical subjects, hampered successful retraining (86).

Another more striking example of retraining for high-skilled and technicians jobs is the participation of the Nuclear Division of the Union Carbide Corporation in the Training and Technology Project begun in June 1966, sponsored by the Oak Ridge Associated Universities with funding by the Manpower Administration of the Department of Labor. Young applicants, mostly high school graduates who earlier had been in low-skilled jobs, were given forty-two weeks of in-plant training and classroom instruction in mechanical drafting, machining of metals, industrial electronics, physical testing-quality control, and laboratory glass blowing. The theoretical and trade-related courses were given by the Tennessee Division of Vocational Technical Education; and mem-

---

* This conclusion supports the findings of an earlier study which reported that by 1965, there were 800 accredited schools for medical technologists located in hospitals, medical schools, boards of health, etc. Yet this study also concluded that there was a sluggish response to shortages because of the relative inflexibility of the training paths for medical technologists and licensed practical nurses (45).

bers of the University of Tennessee staff helped train the teachers, and also provided counseling, guidance, and extensive supportive services for the trainees. During the succeeding three years, 834 were trained (a quarter of them Negroes), and the dropout rate declined from 22 percent in the first group to 9 percent in the last. About 95 percent were still employed at last reporting, and earning an average of $6,333 per year as compared with pre-training average earnings on their last job of $3,577. The cost of training and allowances averaged $3,890 per trainee, but the benefits in earnings and retention rates were also correspondingly high (37).

A laboratory-technician training program, primarily for Negro high school graduates lacking the levels of competence ordinarily required in elementary mathematics, basic chemistry, and English usage was developed at the Procter & Gamble Company in 1968–69. Trainees spent half their time in classroom activities, and half in on-the-job training in laboratory situations learning more about the technician's job. Twenty-five of the twenty-six participants completed the formal instructional program, which had numerous tests and quizzes, and all were offered regular employment as technician trainees. Subsequently, seventeen remained in the company (89, 61).

These formal training programs, however, may be exceptions to the general practice. A survey of training programs for a number of firms in St. Louis and Chicago prior to 1968 showed that only 20 percent trained electronic technicians and 38 percent trained metal technicians, largely through on-the-job training, after specialized training in technical schools and colleges. In commenting on the flexibility of education, training, and experience in the development of technicians and similar skilled employees, the study concluded:

These flexible and relatively informal entry, education and training routes seem to work because of the large number of persons in our society who, while employed in lower levels, have sufficient amounts of college level or technical education as well as mechanical knowledge and aptitudes to enable them to be easily trained for upgraded technical posts (45).

65

These flexible and relatively informal entry, education and training routes seem to work because of the large number of persons in our society who, while employed in lower levels, have sufficient amounts of college level or technical education as well as mechanical knowledge and aptitudes to enable them to be easily trained for upgraded technical posts (45).

Although technicians are probably considered more skilled and of higher status than skilled manual workers, research has indicated that "in many ways they are a marginal group in industry. They lack a clear-cut sense of occupational and professional identification . . ." (72.) In industry, they fall between engineers and production workers; in health services between doctors and other professionals and the low-skilled employees such as orderlies, food service personnel, and others. The study of engineering technicians indicated that they value most highly freedom to use their own judgment and initiative in doing their work.

Another aspect of utilization of technicians relates to the ratio of technicians to engineers and scientists. Technicians would probably have more opportunity to develop their own judgment if the ratio were higher than it is. But in this country, and most others, the ratio is much less than one to one. In 1966, for example, there were only sixty-nine technicians for every one hundred engineers and scientists in private industry. In specific industries, the ratios were higher—above one-to-one in lumber and furniture, other transportation equipment, railroads, telecommunications, radio and TV, and medical and dental laboratories (124). But the average low ratios suggest an underutilization of professionals and an over-supervision of technicians and other subprofessionals.

Engineers

The predicted shortage in the supply of engineers nationally, relative to projected demand, has already been mentioned, as have the hazards of long-range forecasting. We noted earlier that recent cutbacks in defense and space budgets have resulted in layoffs of large numbers of engineers in cities where these operations were concentrated. Up to 1968 and even 1969, however, the demand for beginning engineers continued strong, as evidenced by the ratios of average monthly starting salaries of graduates of other degree fields to engineering graduates (124). As for future supply, the most recent and exhaustive study of professional manpower concludes:

> Since the evidence indicates that the number of students dropping out of engineering has grown in recent years, it is likely that the basic pressures which have limited the growth of engineering in the past will continue to operate in the future . . . The prospects for meeting the demand for engineers at the bachelor's level are very poor (41).

Where are engineers employed? According to a special survey of the employment and other characteristics of a sample of 438,000 engineers who are members of professional and technical societies, 70 percent are employed in private industry, and 4 percent more are self-employed. The federal government and military employ 10 percent; education and nonprofit groups 6 percent; and state and local government 5 percent (the remaining 3 percent are "no report or other") (146). Electrical, mechanical, civil, and chemical engineers predominated, in that order. Only 12 percent were twenty-nine years of age or under. The largest employing industries (in order) were: construction, electrical and electronics products, "services" (transportation, education, communications, etc.), aircraft and spacecraft, and chemical products. Seventy percent of all the engineers surveyed had a bachelor's degree; 22 percent a master's and 5 percent a doctor's degree. Although other data suggest that a large number of those who are classified as "engineers" lack a college degree and have been upgraded earlier (124), only 3 percent of those in this survey reported less than a bachelor's degree (or no report).

It is clear that once engineers are employed in private industry, they do not necessarily remain in the area of their special field of training in college. For example, a study of the proportion of full-time employed 1958 bachelor's degree recipients who changed occupations between 1960 and 1963 showed that nearly 5 percent shifted occupations with the same employer and another 15.5 percent shifted to a different occupation with a different employer. Another 14.2 percent indicated in 1963 that they planned a change in their current occupations (41).

Many engineers tend to move into managerial positions, either in the management of project groups or in more general management. In the survey group of professional engineers referred to earlier, the largest single subgroup (21 percent) reported that they were employed in "management, administration, or technical supervision." Fifteen percent were in research and development, and the same percentage in design. Twelve percent were in "consulting and construction," and 10 percent in "production maintenance, quality control, testing, etc."(146).

This factual review suggests that once engineers are employed in private industry, there is considerable "on-the-job training," most of it fairly informal, through working with other engineers and under the direction of managers. Some firms, such as General Electric, have had more formal post-graduate training programs within the company for young engineering graduates. Many others provide tuition refunds for those who take further formal higher education at nearby colleges and universities.

Another problem is the effective utilization of engineers. The literature on the management of professional manpower, particularly those in research and development (including scientists) is vast (121, 79). Colleague-management, rather than superior-subordinate management, seems to be more effective. Another aspect is the ratio of technicians to engineers. As we have noted earlier, this ratio is considerably less than one-to-one in most industries. The productivity of engineers in industry can be increased "by reorganizing specific engineering jobs so that the less skilled personnel take over the routine duties and the highly trained engineer can concentrate on the more complex problems . . ." (41) This assumes, of course, that the supply of technicians can be increased faster than the supply of engineers, and requires a relatively greater expansion of the educational programs for technicians. The problem that industry has in attracting young graduate engineers is related to the nature of their starting jobs, because there "is the rather widespread belief held by youth of college age that engineers are seldom assigned challenging jobs" (124).

Older employed engineers, however, increasingly need new knowledge to keep abreast of rapid changes in technology in their fields and the development of wholly new fields of application. According to a study of thirty-nine firms by Norgren, the problem is largely confined to about 25 percent of the professional and technical work force—those over thirty-five who work primarily in research and development. In-plant training programs and tuition refund plans for outside formal study are ways in which firms have dealt with the problem, but the lack of basic math and science backgrounds, as well as family and community responsibilities and lack of motivation, have limited the number who can take advantage of further higher education after thirty-five (109). This is confirmed by another study of the unemployment and job finding experience of engineers (and some scientists) laid off by eight electronics firms in the Boston area in 1965 as a result of cutbacks in defense contracts. Many of these were men whose education had been completed ten years earlier, who had not taken further formal education, and whose backgrounds in mathematics and science subjects were relatively weaker than those still employed (90).

A study of seventeen research and development laboratories (of which nine were in private industry) and 250 research and development scientists and engineers showed that scientists were more motivated toward continuing education than were engineers. Both scientists and engineers preferred the following activities, in the order listed: in-lab lectures or seminars, attendance at professional meetings, in-lab formal courses (non-credit), outside university credit courses, short intensive courses, and educational leaves of absence with pay. Employer policies tended to stress expenses paid to meetings, outside courses with tuition refunds, sabbatical leaves with pay (for selected employees only) and in-lab lectures (23).

Another study of 290 scientists and engineers employed in aerospace and nuclear plants and in government laboratories reached somewhat different conclusions about how to deal with technological obsolescence of professionals. On-the-job training, including new and challenging assignments to varied projects, was stressed. "Such opportunities are largely a function of the organizational environment and, specifically, the degree to which the institution facilitates or restrains the continual appraisal of specific areas which require development for each individual" (80). Formal educational opportunities are most useful as a part of this on-the-job development.

SOME UNANSWERED QUESTIONS

1. How valid are the projections that there will be serious shortages in technicians and in engineers by 1975 or 1980? What would continuing studies in particular firms or industries show about the way in which these shortages were overcome, assuming that supply does not increase faster or the demand increase less than the projections now indicate?

2. Is there any further evidence or experience with the better utilization of professional engineers and scientists through increasing the number of technicians working with them?

3. To what extent have firms improved the nature of initial job assignments for new graduate engineers to make them more challenging, and to reduce the turnover of young engineers?

6

Management Training and Development

The private sector of the economy is clearly the largest employer of management talent. Thus, management training and development is seen as meeting the continuing shortage of good managers. The literature on this subject is large and growing, but a good deal of it is in fairly general terms, consisting of "principles" or general statements about how effective managers and top executives are developed.

A recent report on top management development in a number of companies followed a review of the state of knowledge on this subject by the Business Education Committee and the Business-Education Advisory Board of the Committee for Economic Development. The foreword notes the following conclusions from the discussion:

There is a wealth of pious statements in the literature about what companies are doing, based on what they *think* they are doing. But there is often a disparity between this and what is actually being done.

Many companies appear to think of management development as something that is done to the individual rather than as a step in a continuous and integrated management process, involving not only the motives and development of the individuals but likewise the philosophy, objectives, and organizational structure of the corporation . . .

The corporate environment, which embodies the formal authority system, policies and practices, the control system, and the wages and jobs set by the organizational structure, is created by top management. Hence, development must begin at the very top, and if change is needed, that must also occur at the top . . . (51).

C.E.D. sponsored an "exploratory study" to determine how people are selected for top management positions; it was based on the practice of thirteen large corporations that have had some success in management development (51). Some twelve conclusions emerged from this study, but the two committees were most impressed with the following: "1) Development and succession of top management is not simply an extension of the process that operates at lower levels of management; 2) selection for the top ranks of a large corporation depends on being identified at an early stage in one's career and remaining continuously visible to those who select their successors; 3) the selection of executives is a process that extends over a long period of time; and 4) there is practically no solid information available to evaluate the methods of top management development and succession" (51; 139).

The last conclusion is perhaps the most interesting, in view of the widespread belief in the importance of management training and development. An earlier study concluded that formal education prior to entering a management career will be less important to total experience and continuing development as a manager approaches the age when top management leadership is in sight, and it stressed the responsibility of industry for developing and making effective use of mature executives (10). If top executives develop and select their successors, therefore, there is a tendency for them to advance people like themselves, who have similar values. The "gatekeepers" establish both the climate for management development and the conditions under which the gates are opened to those striving for the top. Evaluation of results, therefore, is difficult, for successes may be self-fulfilling prophecies, and failures the exceptions seldom mentioned and moved sidewise, if not separated in some fashion.

Some research has been done on factors affecting promotion to top management ranks in industry. Patten found that subordinate managers are not likely to get ahead if they are good merely in "human relations" or in solving routine problems. Higher management is seeking those who have the ability to solve critical, nonroutine problems (114). A study of graduates of the School of Industrial Administration at Carnegie-Mellon showed that those who have been most successful were highly motivated, technically competent, sensitive to their work environment, and able to adapt to changing work assignments and environments (29).

Increasingly, today's managers, including first-line supervisors (63), tend to be college graduates. Possibly those who have an undergraduate degree in engineering, economics, or business have a slight edge, especially engineers with graduate business training in manufacturing or research-based organizations. Graduate work in business administration has increasingly appealed to students and business firms hiring them as a desirable educational preparation for a career in management. But perhaps even more popular is the view that at some point in a manager's development, he needs "broadening" through a university management development program. Such programs may not be seen as qualifying a man for promotion to higher management, but rather as further preparing him for these responsibilities (51).

UNIVERSITY MANAGEMENT DEVELOPMENT PROGRAMS

Since World War II there has been a rapid spread of university-sponsored management development programs for practicing managers. One of the best known is a thirteen-week Advanced Management Program at the Graduate School of Business Administration of Harvard University, although the oldest continuing program is the Sloan Fellows Program for younger managers with top management potential, at the Sloan School of Management,

M.I.T. Most programs, however are shorter than the one-year Sloan program at M.I.T.; they average two to thirteen weeks.

Several studies have been made of the experience with university-sponsored management development programs. One by Kenneth Andrews of the Harvard Business School found that 94 percent of 6,000 graduates of thirty-nine university programs between 1948 and 1959 welcomed the opportunity to attend (usually at the request of their company) and saw their selection as indication of their company's recognition of their ability and hence their promotability (3). Four fifths responded very favorably at the end of the program they attended; many termed it "the single most important experience of their professional lives" (3). Classroom activities and study for class were rated higher than social intercourse.

Andrews admitted that he was unable to measure the specific contribution of the programs either to individual performance back on the job or to subsequent cost-saving for the company. But he stressed the value of these programs as seen by the respondents themselves in terms of their own personal broadenings:

> We see once again that the impact of the university program has been to turn a man's attention upon himself rather than to the processes of business as such or to the nature of the world around him. Sixty-two percent of those counted reported change in the perception, interest, attitudes, and activities principally with respect to themselves as individuals (self) or as businessmen (job) (3).

A later study of these programs is more descriptive and less analytical than Andrews' (159). Recent changes in program content have emphasized quantitative and systems analysis, behavioral sciences, and the organization-society interface. Company objectives in sending managers to these programs (as reported by thirty-five major firms) are to broaden managers as preparation for additional responsibility, provide them with the latest information on business theory and practice, stimulate innovation and creativity, provide an opportunity to interact with other managers, and given them time to assess their personal career development.

But nothing in the study indicates whether companies attempted to evaluate the extent to which these objectives were realized, and none of the managers attending these programs were interviewed. The primary consideration for selection of participants by companies was said to be the person's promotability and his age—preferably in the thirty-five-to-fifty range.

It is a reasonable conclusion from the available evidence that while the results for the company may be difficult or impossible to evaluate, both the companies and the men who attend these programs seem to be satisfied that there is mutual benefit, primarily in the "broadening" of the manager at an important stage of his upward career. But it is also clear that these programs can only supplement and not supplant the development of managers *within* the organization. As Andrews pointed out, "If the executive program [at the university] is to have a long-range effect, its stimulation must be extended. It must be incorporated into the organization processes which affect individual behavior and influence it significantly in one of two directions: accomplishment, growth, innovation and professional excellence, on the one hand, or decline, reaction and mediocrity on the other (3; 84, 75, 76). The organizational climate, supportive rather than restrictive, is all-important for managerial self-development.

Association and In-Company Management Programs

Similar observations may be made about programs run by various management associations such as the American Management Association, Industrial Relations Counselors, or the research-oriented National Industrial Conference Board. These are usually much shorter in duration than most university-based programs, and often tend to emphasize functional areas, such as marketing, production management, industrial relations and personnel administration, as well as general management. No evaluation studies of these programs have been made, but it may be assumed that their value lies in "broadening" the manager attending, exposing him to some new knowledge, and giving him the benefit of an

75

exchange of ideas with other practicing managers. Until recently, at least, these programs were generally well filled: the American Management Association, with 61,000 members, is reported to have offered as many as 2,300 seminars and meetings each year (17, 5).

The National Training Laboratory pioneered a special type of "management training"—sensitivity training, known also as "laboratory training," or the T-group approach. A recent review of research on this method, now often combined with training in "organization development," indicates "clear evidence" that personal growth results for most participants, but that the value for subsequent job performance is less convincing (15; 130). But in studies of effective and ineffective organization development efforts, laboratory training was not found to be a crucial variable; what was important was "the introduction of new and fruitful concepts of diagnosing current problems of organization and setting improvement goals" (15).

A few firms have used laboratory training for successive levels of management within the organization. But for the most part, in-company management training programs provide larger numbers of managers with exposure to some of the same body of knowledge and concepts offered by the outside programs in management associations and in universities. For example, from 1956 to 1961, the General Electric Company had an Advanced Management Course attended by about 1,500 executives in a residential center at Crotonville, New York. There was considerable emphasis on company indoctrination and exposure to different functional top managers. In January 1964, the New General Management Course replaced the earlier one and emphasized more material on the business environment (with outside lecturers) and on case studies (48). In 1969, Western Electric opened a residential corporate education center, which offered some 300 courses taught by 120 educators in two major areas: engineering and business management. At higher management levels, the business environment was stressed; at lower levels, planning, supervision, and relations among departments and divisions (77). No objective evaluations of these programs have been published, although the fact that substantial funds (including executive time) are devoted by profit-making enterprises to them suggests some concept of net return.

Most other business firms, however, have less formal programs of management and executive development. Whether the responsibility is initially centered in the personnel department or in a separate department, the staff function helps top management keep track of promotable as well as potentially promotable managers to fill vacancies created by other promotions, retirements, deaths, and voluntary terminations to take management in other firms. Decisions are made about rotation to other management jobs within the organization to gain broader experience, attendance at shorter outside seminars or conferences, nomination for a university management development program, special assignments, membership in project groups, etc. Considerations are given to forecasts of managerial requirements over time, and in particular divisions of profit centers. All of this increases the visibility of middle managers to top management, which has the final responsibility for replacing itself, as noted earlier, as well as for staffing lower key managerial posts.

"Experience and research generally affirm the proposition that greater mobility of managers increases the range of choice and flexibility in the deployment of human resources and most often results in a more adaptable organization" (51). But it may also be important to ask whether mobility required of individual managers has offsetting costs, and whether some choice in the decision to move now, and if so, where, should be offered to the manager himself (2). In either case, it is obvious that in developing managers there is considerable on-the-job training, working under a succession of higher managers (51).

RECRUITMENT OF BLACK GRADUATES; BLACKS IN MANAGEMENT

Within the past five years or more, many businesses have made a special effort to recruit black college graduates, and particularly those with master's degrees in business administration and management. It is said by many managers that any qualified black will have a number of business offers.

However, a number of surveys and other analyses of the degree of penetration of blacks in management suggests that they still have a long way to go. For example, a 1969 study of a sample of eighty-six black MBA's who were graduated over the preceding eighteen years (with an average age of twenty-nine) showed that only 8 percent are known to have an annual salary of more than $11,000 (38). The author of this study suggested that the positive attitude of top management toward black recruitment and promotion had not penetrated far enough down the line, since the department head level in particular was not demonstrating much positive action.

As for blacks in the executive group, a study by a black management recruiting agency indicated that early in 1969 there were less than thirty black corporate executives earning more than $30,000 a year (99). A later review notes that many black department heads or vice presidents are not given mainstream positions in their companies; instead they can be found in public relations, community or urban affairs, special markets, or equal employment opportunities (8; 53).

Another analysis of 441 Plans for Progress companies, employing 936,512 managers and officials, claimed that only 1.1 percent of these were black. (The percentage of professionals was only slightly higher—1.4 percent) (137). In the aerospace industry in 1966, Northrup found only four tenths of 1 percent of those classified as "officials and managers" were black, and most then were first-line supervisors. But he added that business recruiters are actually pursuing black candidates, especially those from aerospace companies (111). Nevertheless, the progress from the standpoint of blacks in business is disappointingly slow.

What is needed, according to James S. Spain, to reduce "corporate racism" is recruitment of qualifiable as well as qualified blacks at all management levels, creation of an inventory of the supervisory and managerial potential of blacks so that progress can be audited on a regular basis (which would also serve to evaluate the effectiveness of training efforts by white managers), a policy of accelerated promotion for blacks to close the gap proportionately between blacks and whites in management, and a special management development seminar including all black managers and professionals (136). He also calls for regular reports from field offices and plants to corporate headquarters on progress in employing and upgrading blacks in management and on utilization of black management recruiting firms.

In a longer run effort, the Alfred P. Sloan Foundation has allotted $1 million for fellowships and counseling blacks in graduate schools of business, and has funded a Council of Opportunities in Graduate Management Education representing ten top business schools. An earlier Ford Foundation-financed consortium of five graduate business schools awarded sixty-five fellowships to blacks in 1969–70 (102). These efforts will unodubtedly increase the supply of potential black executives, but in the meantime the management training and development efforts reviewed earlier in this main section need to be applied with special force to those blacks already in the management ranks.

SOME UNANSWERED QUESTIONS

This review of the literature of management training and development suggests further questions for study:

1. If there is now little or no solid evidence to evaluate the methods of top management development and succession, including that part involved in university management development programs, how can this gap be overcome? Is it possible to design a research study which is not plagued by the problems of interdependence of factors, including the possibility that those selected early for advancement may not be superior to those overlooked (138)? Possibly a study which matched firms by industry, size, and other characteristics, but differed greatly in their management development efforts, would throw some light on the relative costs and benefits of such programs.

2. How important is the managerial climate, stressed in so many studies and management literature? Can this be objectively tested, by extensive questionnaire and/or interview studies of a number of firms, or a number of managers in a single firm (129)?

3. Is management development really self-development through the motivation of an individual manager to prepare himself for advancement by the way in which he performs his job and takes advantage of rotation opportunities and association or university management programs? Or is the initiative largely on the part of the man's superior and with top management?

4. What is the relative value of these two approaches from the standpoint of manager motivation and development? Would more initiative with the manager improve his development as a competent manager, or not?

5. What can be done, within the general management training and development effort of the firm to advance black managers? What would be the impact on other managers if black managers were accelerated faster? Would this be understood as providing equal opportunity for advancement by overcoming existing discrimination, as is claimed? Does top management commitment need to be implemented more forcefully among middle and supervisory management? A study of a number of firms on these questions is needed.

7

Private-for-Profit Training and Vocational Schools

Prior to seeking employment in private firms, a large number of people apparently look for training and vocational education in private-for-profit schools, which are separate from the public educational system and largely uncontrolled by state or federal government. There have been only a few studies of this type of training, and it clearly deserves more careful scrutiny in the future.

One earlier estimate put the number of private schools of this type at around 35,000 with some 5 million students enrolled, but some of these offered leisure time activities (such as art and music) as well as employment-related courses (20). A more recently survey by Belitsky stated that there were 7,000 private schools offering vocational training to about 1.5 million students (7). The variation in these estimates indicates the gaps in our knowledge about a neglected area in private-sector training. A 1964 government-sponsored study listed "special schools" as the most important source of training for accountants and auditors, artists and art teachers, barbers, hairdressers and cosmetologists, office machine operators, practical nurses, professional nurses, and welders and flamecutters. These schools were listed as an important secondary source for nine other occupations, including secretaries, and medical and dental technicians (152). The same study also lists correspondence schools, many of which are private, as the most important source of training for radio and television mechanics, and an important secondary source for accountants and auditors, artists and art teachers, and technicians in engineering and physical sciences. Some of these seem a little surprising.

One of the most common type of private-for-profit schools is in the "trade and technical" classification, according to Belitsky. He studied a sample of 544 out of the 3,000 schools in this group, and found that courses in data processing, electronics, and medical services were the most numerous. In data processing, there were more courses offered for "data processors" (including keypunch and tab operators) than for programmers or computer maintenance workers. Belitsky found that the emphasis in most schools is on a concrete and job-related institutional setting. About one third of the students in the trade and technical area were high school dropouts.

However, in the computer field as well as in some others, promises seem to have exceeded performance. For example, a study in New York City found that apart from computer manufacturers, which were the largest single training resource, a number of students attended fee-charging private schools. There were many negative comments made about these schools by employers, technicians, and personnel experts. These criticisms centered on the quality of the training, the instructors, and the obsolete equipment. "They were accused of taking anybody's money and enrolling students who were obviously unfit or unqualified for the occupation selected. To make matters worse, many schools implied guaranteed placement for their graduates, a guarantee which was evaded in the small print and which could not be met" (161). In Boston, a private computer school closed abruptly in January 1970, leaving stranded nearly two hundred students, who had paid from $700 to $1800 for tuition (11, 108). Local insurance firms expressed an interest in some of them, without further schooling.

Franke and Sobel's study in St. Louis and Chicago included in the technical trade group private schools which trained tool and die makers and electronic technicians. Of the eleven technician schools in their survey, seven were private. Many were operating below capacity (45), possibly because they were in competition with free public vocational schools.

Medical assistants were being trained in at least 250 private schools in 1968, according to a spokesman for the National Association of Trade and Technical Schools. However, Franke and Sobel report that only 5 percent of the hospital supervisors in their St. Louis-Chicago survey gave a "good" or better rating to these private schools, based on the performance of their graduates. Criticism also was made of facilities, low admission standards, poor teachers, and lack of interest in the students (45).

Private business and commercial schools are also numerous. Six of the thirty-nine private-for-profit schools studied in Santa Clara County, California (71), were in this category, and 90 percent of their students were women, of whom two thirds were between seventeen and twenty-two years of age, mostly with a high school diploma. Ten of the thirty-nine were cosmetology and barber schools, in which three fourths of the students were under twenty-three years of age. Eight schools were classed as trade and technical; the course content was directly related to the prospective job. Six were in "real estate" with most students in a four-to-six-week training program for salesmen.

Another type of private-for-profit school has sprung up recently to assist private industry in training the disadvantaged for productive employment. Primarily, these schools offer pre-employment training to remedy educational deficiencies in applicants, and they are used when private employers have contracts with the Manpower Administration of the Department of Labor through the NAB-JOBS program. One of the most publicized of these companies is MIND, Inc., which was first established in 1967 as a wholly owned subsidiary of Corn Products Company (now CPA International, Inc.). By 1968, it had some 130 companies as clients, including IBM, American Express, Consolidated Edison, Continental Can, and Xerox (19).

The MIND program has no classrooms or teachers, using instead conference tables, basic-education workbooks, tapes, etc., with nonprofessionals as classroom helpers. Courses include math and literacy skills, typing, and stenography. Some earlier clients have been dissatisfied with results, and at least one (Consolidated Edison) has gone back to classroom teachers for basic pre-employment education.

Finally, among the private-for-profit training and vocational schools are those that offer instruction only by correspondence. The International Correspondence School and the LaSalle Extension University (the latter now part of Crowell-Collier Publishing Company) are among the oldest and best known, but there are many more. Estimates run from 500 to 1,000, some of which belong to an Association of Home Study Schools. Probably as many as 2.5 million "customers" pay far less than $100 to more than $2,500 for some type of instruction mailed to their homes. Apparently, heavy promotion budgets are needed to generate this number of users.*

The use of questionable practices, including large salesmen's commissions, has led another trade group, the National Home Study Council, to establish minimum standards for business and education operations. Only 133 schools have been accredited by this group; the majority of private correspondence schools are not members.

This brief review of private-for-profit schools in general indicates the paucity of our knowledge about them. Many in the trade and technical area, as well as in business and commercial fields, are probably reasonably successful. But the size of the industry is subject to wide variations in estimates, and not much is really known about the effectiveness of these schools relative to public vocational schools in placing graduates or, with exceptions noted earlier, in the performance of graduates as seen by subsequent employers. This whole area deserves wider exploration.

* Walter Rugaber, "Mail Order Students are Found Plagued by Dubious Practices," *New York Times*, July 31, 1970, p. 1. For a more extensive discussion of correspondence schools, see Ossian MacKenzie, Edward L. Christensen, and Paul H. Rigby, *Correspondence Instruction in the United States* (New York: McGraw-Hill Book Company, 1968).

8

Summary and Conclusions

The preceding sections have reviewed the experience of the private sector in the U.S. economy in developing manpower. Since private firms account for three fourths to four fifths of employment in the non-farm economy (depending on the measures used), it is clear that they are *the* major source of trained manpower in the U.S. labor force.

This is not to deny the prior role of the educational system in preparing young people for the world of work, even though this preparation may be inadequate in some cases (especially for minorities) and the transition is not always smooth (148). But the relationship between general educational background, specific vocational preparation, and occupational skill level is well-established. As years of general education and specific vocational preparation increase, annual earnings and the job content level also increase (131). What the private employer does is to build on this educational background, including in some cases specific vocational education, by training, motivating, and developing the employee on the job and over his working lifetime with one or several different employers. Employees also make an investment in their own training, by taking less pay on prior jobs or in apprenticeship programs as they seek *to qualify themselves for better jobs.*

Obviously, some employers invest more in training and development of their human resources than do others, and there is often a gap between what the better firms do and what the average firm does. A period of labor shortage, represented by expansion of employment in particular firms or industries, and by a full-employment economy, will force more private firms to invest in training and upgrading employees at all levels than in periods when experienced employees are seeking work and can be hired at various "ports of entry" in the occupational structure without much further training on the job.

The importance of more or less informal on-the-job training for production and some maintenance jobs has been shown in the research studies reviewed earlier. Skilled mechanical crafts and those in the construction industry frequently require some more formal apprenticeship training along with on-the-job training, but many workers arrive at craftsmen or journeymen status through informal routes. Apprenticeship programs in construction have generally been a method by which all-round craftsmen able to command the union rate could be developed, although restriction of entry to minorities has often been charged.

People with labor market disadvantages, in terms of poor education and little or no previous regular employment, or victims of discrimination have a more difficult time finding steady employment with prospects for upgrading and promotion within the enterprise. A number of large firms, prior to the more recent nationwide effort, reported successful experiences in recruiting, hiring, and training the disadvantaged. Beginning early in 1968, the government-financed JOBS program of the National Alliance of Business was launched, with ambitious targets for mid-1970 and 1971. There is considerable evidence that this program induced more firms than before to make a hiring and training commitment, but the full employment economy through most of 1969 undoubtedly helped. Critics of this effort now have their innings, but it is difficult to avoid the conclusion that some net benefit to the disadvantaged as well as to future employment of this group has resulted from encouraging private firms to re-examine their recruiting efforts, hiring standards, training methods, and personnel policies generally. Public subsidies, through contracts rather than tax incentives, are justified in offsetting additional training costs which are incurred, if further employment of the disadvantaged in the private sector is a national manpower goal. But careful monitoring of such contracts is warranted, and more information should be secured on the performance of non-contract firms.

The record of construction craft unions, spurred by government and other pressures, in opening apprenticeship programs to minority applicants is mixed, but considerable progress has been made in some localities and by some unions. As in the case of the NAB-JOBS program, progress in hiring more of the disadvantaged in the private sector requires a combination of pressures, persuasion, and successful experience. The interface of private and public efforts is a new development of the late 1960's, and will undoubtedly continue. Support for such other private groups as the Urban League and Opportunities Industrialization Centers is an important part of this effort.

Some of these programs also affect white-collar jobs, particularly those in the clerical, stenographic, secretarial, data processing, and office machine operation occupations. Most white-collar jobs, however, seem to be built on prior educational background involving a high school degree or, in some cases, junior or community college. Even here, the amount of subsequent on-the-job training provided by many employers varies from a few weeks to many months. Promotion from blue-collar to white-collar jobs with on-the-job training is rare, but a growing possibility for some jobs.

Post-high school education, up to the Ph.D. for research engineers and scientists, is usually required for many technical and professional jobs. The prospect is that technical and professional manpower shortages will face the private sector (as well as the nonprofit and public sectors) in the next decade, despite the current phenomenon of unemployment. As in the case of many other white-collar jobs, new employees often receive further on-the-job training, usually informal but supplemented by formal seminars, tuition support for outside university courses, and in the case of engineers and scientists particularly, expenses for attendance at professional meetings where new knowledge is acquired and new colleagues met. More effective utilization of talented technical and professional manpower is a neglected area of management concern and research study. So is the problem of skill obsolescence among technicians and engineers, some of whom have undoubtedly been released as defense and space programs have been cut back.

Similar problems are found in management and executive development programs, although large firms make extensive use of outside university and management association programs designed to "broaden" prospective top managers. While a college background in engineering and economics-business administration is increasingly a prerequisite for advancement in management ranks, there are some exceptions. More important than prior educational background is the organizational climate within which executives develop by moving to different assignments, assuming additional responsibilities successfully, and taking advantage of outside opportunities to improve their managerial skills and knowledge. Non-whites managers are few, but many large firms have sought able graduates of colleges and business schools to help meet the shortages of competent managers, as well as to avoid charges of discrimination.

A separate area of the private sector—private-for-profit training schools and programs—contributes to the development of manpower in particular occupations such as secretarial, trade and technical, and barbering and hairdressing. Private schools also train for computer-related and aviation jobs. Most are fee-charging classroom and job-training schools; but there is an important sector that sells instruction by correspondence. Comparatively little is known about this whole area of training, and more study is needed.

88

Although the private sector's role in the economy is still by far the largest, the public and nonprofit sectors are growing. In the latter are institutions of higher education, research laboratories, foundations, religious organizations, and many others. Government services of all kinds, public education, public hospitals, public enterprises such as TVA, and the armed services comprise the bulk of the public sector, which has been growing relative to the private sector over the past decade. We have already seen how the federal government has subsidized training efforts in the private sector for the disadvantaged. Public subsidy of public employment of the disadvantaged has been started within recent years through the New Careers Program and the later Public Service Careers program.

To the extent that there are unmet manpower needs in the not-for-profit and public sectors of the economy, the private sector can contribute little other than by losing trained manpower to these other sectors as salary levels and the stability of employment represented by Civil Service appear more attractive to prospective employees. Most of the manpower needs will be met through the recruitment, training, and development efforts of public and nonprofit agencies and their managers. If budgets dependent on tax revenues are tight, just as the private sector is similarly affected by a decline in demand, further subsidies to provide training (for existing job vacancies) may be necessary. But the usual proposal involves relatively more emphasis on the supply side, in providing public employment "as a last resort" for those who are unable to find employment in the larger private sector.

While the public subsidy of additional jobs in the public and non-private sector may be justified on an expanded basis, the direct public subsidy of jobs in the private sector is clearly unthinkable, except where government requires products or services from the private sector, as in defense and space programs. At most, there is a case for public subsidy of *additional costs* of training and bringing to productive levels of employment those individuals who have serious labor market disadvantages in finding good jobs in the large private sector.

89

As we have seen, this may involve contracts (subsidies) with individual firms directly, or it may involve subsidized training programs in such nonprofit organizations as OIC or the Urban League, or with other private training firms. The eventual objective of these publicly subsidized programs, as in the institutional training programs established under the MDTA and subsidized union training programs, is employment in the private sector, although not exclusively.

This partnership between the manpower programs funded by the federal government and firms in the private sector is likely to continue, so long as there is emphasis on employing the disadvantaged. Whether these expenditures will stand the test of rigorous cost-benefit analyses is for the most part an unanswered question, but the preliminary evidence reviewed in this study is, on balance, favorable.

To date, the public-private partnership in training has not really extended to the other occupational groups reviewed earlier, except when federal contracts cover training costs, as in aerospace. The newer issue of a federal government obligation to those engineers, scientists, and technicians who were employed in earlier high-priority national programs now cut back with the resulting high-talent manpower wastage, is under current discussion. One possibility is a retraining component in new federal research and development contracts with private firms, but this raises still other questions about similar opportunities for less-favored occupational groups similarly affected.

For the most part, it is in the self-interest of firms in the private sector to train, develop, and retrain their own high-talent manpower, as well as those with other skills required by efficient enterprises. The gaps in our knowledge about the specific methods used, and the relative success of these methods, suggest the need for further studies of this experience.

References

1. *A Policy for Skilled Manpower.* National Manpower Council. New York: Columbia University Press, 1954.
2. Alfred, Theodore M. "Checkers or Choice in Manpower Management," *Harvard Business Review,* vol. 45, no. 1 (January–February, 1967), pp. 157–167.
3. Andrews, Kenneth R. *The Effectiveness of University Management Development Programs.* Division of Research, Graduate School of Business Administration. Boston, 1966.
4. Banfield, Edward C. "An Act of Corporate Citizenship," in *Programs to Employ the Disadvantaged* ed. by Peter B. Doeringer. Englewood Cliffs, N.J.: Prentice Hall, Inc., 1969.
5. Basil, Douglas C. *Executive Comparison of Small and Large Enterprises.* Minneapolis: University of Minnesota, 1964.
6. Beaumont, Richard A., and Roy B. Helfgott. *Management, Automation, and People.* Industrial Relations Monograph No. 24, Industrial Relations Counselors. New York, 1964.
7. Belitsky, A. Harvey. *Private Vocational Schools and Their Students: Limited Objectives, Unlimited Opportunities.* Cambridge, Mass.: Schenkman Publishing Company, 1969.
8. Bender, Marylin. "Blacks Snubbed in Business," *New York Times,* April 19, 1970.
9. Bok, Derek C., and John T. Dunlop. *Labor and the American Community.* New York: Simon and Schuster, 1970.
10. Bond, F. A., D. A. Leabo, and A. W. Swinyard. *Preparations for Business Leadership: Views of Top Executives.* Michigan Business

Report No. 43, Bureau of Business Research, Graduate School of Business Administration, University of Michigan. Ann Arbor, Michigan, 1964.

11. *Boston Globe*, January 23, 1970.

12. *Boston Herald Traveller*, July 4, 1970.

13. *Boston Herald Traveller*, July 28, 1970.

14. Briggs, Vernon M. Jr., "The Negro in American Industry: A Review of Seven Studies," *Journal of Human Resources*, vol. 5, no. 3 (Summer, 1970), pp. 370–381.

15. Buchanan, Paul C. "Laboratory Training and Organization Development," *Administrative Science Quarterly*, vol. 14, no. 3 (September, 1969), pp. 466–480.

16. *Business Amid Urban Crises*. Studies in Public Affairs No. 3. New York: National Industrial Conference Board, 1968.

17. *Business Week*. May 23, 1970.

18. *Business Week*. May 30, 1970.

19. Carlson, Elliott. "Education and Industry: Troubled Partnership," *Saturday Review*, vol. 53, no. 33 (August 15, 1970), pp. 45–47, 58–60.

20. Clark, Harold F., and Harold S. Sloan. *Classrooms on Main Street*. New York: Teachers College Press, 1966.

21. Cohn, Jules. "Is Business Meeting the Challenge of Urban Affairs?," *Harvard Business Review*, vol. 48, no. 2 (March–April, 1970), pp. 68–82.

22. ———. *The Conscience of Corporation*. Baltimore: The Johns Hopkins Press, 1970.

23. *Continuing Education for R & D Careers*. National Science Foundation, NSF 69–20. Prepared by Social Research, Inc., Chicago, Illinois. Washington, D.C., June 1969.

24. Corwin, R. David. "New Yorkers in the Banking Industry: A Minority Report." New York: Department of Sociology, New York University, June 1970.

25. Crowley, Michael F. "Projected Requirements for Technicians in 1980," *Monthly Labor Review*, vol. 93, no. 5 (May, 1970), pp. 13–17.

26. *Daily Labor Report*, May 13, 1970, p. 17.

27. Derryck, Dennis A. "Breakthrough in the Building Trades" in *Conference on Upgrading and New Careers*, sponsored by the National Manpower Policy Task Force. Washington, D.C., March, 1970.

28. Diamond, Daniel E., and Hrach Bedrosian. *Hiring Standards and Job Performance*. Prepared for the Department of Labor/Manpower Administration, Manpower Research Monograph No. 18. Washington, D.C.: U.S. Government Printing Office, 1970.

REFERENCES

29. Dill, William R., Thomas L. Hilton, and Walter R. Reitman. *The New Managers*. Englewood Cliffs, N.J.: Prentice-Hall, Inc, 1962.
30. Doeringer, Peter B. (ed.). *Programs to Employ the Disadvantaged*. Englewood Cliffs, N.J.: Prentice-Hall, Inc., 1969.
31. Doeringer, Peter B., and Michael J. Piore. "Equal Employment Opportunity in Boston," *Industrial Relations*, vol. 9, no. 3 (May, 1970), pp. 324–339.
32. ———. *Internal Labor Markets and Manpower Analysis*. Boston: D. C. Heath and Company, 1971.
33. Drattel, Alan, "Preparing the Unskilled for Data Processing," *Business Automation*, vol. 13, no. 1 (January, 1966), pp. 39–40.
34. Dunlop, John T. "Job Vacancy Measures and Economic Analysis," *The Measurement and Interpretation of Job Vacancies*. New York: National Bureau of Economic Research, 1966; distributed by Columbia University Press.
35. ———. "The Nation's Manpower Arrangements: The Directions of Private Policies in the 1970's," *The Conference Board Record*, vol. 7, no. 3 (March, 1970), pp. 27–29.
36. Dunnette, M. D., J. P. Campbell, E. E. Lawler, and K. E. Weick. *Management Effectiveness*. New York: McGraw-Hill Book Company, 1969.
37. Echols, James L. "Technicians: How to Grow Your Own," *Manpower*, vol. 2, no. 1 (January, 1970), pp. 8–12.
38. Fields, Charles L. "Industry's Response to the Black MBA," *The MBA*, vol. 3, no. 7 (April–May, 1969), p. 61.
39. Finley, Grace J. "An Assessment of the Urban Coalition," *The Conference Board Record*, vol. 7, no. 2 (February, 1970), pp. 48–52.
40. Fisher, Lloyd. *The Harvest Labor Market in California*. Cambridge: Harvard University Press, 1953.
41. Folger, John K., Helen S. Astin, and Alan E. Bayer. *Human Resources and Higher Education: Staff Report of the Commission of Human Resources and Advanced Education*. New York: Russell Sage Foundation, 1970.
42. Foltman, Felician F. "An Assessment of Apprenticeship," *Monthly Labor Review*, vol. 87, no. 1 (January, 1964), p. 32.
43. ———. "Xerox Corporation—A Case Study in Retraining," *Management of Personnel Quarterly*, vol. 1, no. 5 (Winter, 1962), p. 19.
44. Foster, Howard G. "Nonapprentice Sources of Training in Construction," *Monthly Labor Review*, vol. 93, no. 2 (February, 1970), pp. 21–26.
45. Franke, Walter, and Irvin Sobel. *The Shortage of Skilled and Tech-*

nical Workers. Institute of Labor and Industrial Relations, University of Illinois. Urbana, Illinois, June, 1968.

46. Freedman, Marcia. *The Process of Work Establishment.* New York: Columbia University, 1969.

47. Fuchs, Victor R. *The Service Economy.* New York: Natioal Bureau of Economic Research, 1968; distributed by Columbia University Press.

48. "G. E.'s 'College' is Back in Session," *Business Week* (February 8, 1964), p. 78.

49. Ginzberg, Eli. "Business Colleges in a Pluralistic Economy." *The Compass* (Official Journal of the United Business Schools Association), vol. 34, no. 2 (February, 1970), p. 9.

50. Ginzberg, Eli, Dale L. Hiestand, and Beatrice G. Reubens. *The Pluralistic Economy.* New York: McGraw-Hill Book Company, 1965.

51. Glickman, Albert S., Clifford P. Hahn, Edwin A. Fleishman, and Brent Baxter (of American Institutes for Research, Washington, D.C.). *Top Management Development and Succession: An Exploratory Study.* Supplementary Paper No. 27, Committee for Economic Development. New York, November, 1968.

52. Goldfarb, Robert S. "The Evaluation of Government Programs: The Case of New Haven's Manpower Training Activities," Unpublished Ph.D. thesis, Department of Economics, Yale University, 1968.

53. Goode, Kenneth C. "Query: Can the Afro-American be an Effective Executive?" *California Management Review,* vol. 13, no. 1 (Fall, 1970), pp. 22–26.

54. Goodman, Paul S. "Hiring, Training, and Retraining the Hard Core," *Industrial Relations,* vol. 9, no. 1 (October, 1969), pp. 54–66.

55. *Government Commitment to Occupational Training in Industry.* Report of the Task Force on Occupational Training in Industry. Washington, D.C.: U.S. Government Printing Office, August, 1968.

56. Greenfield, Harry I. (with the assistance of Carl A. Brown). *Allied Health Manpower.* New York: Columbia University Press, 1969.

57. Grinker, William J., Donald D. Cooke, and Arthur W. Kersch. *Climbing the Job Ladder.* New York: E. F. Shelley & Co., 1970.

58. Haas, Frederick C. *Executive Obsolescence.* Research Study 60. New York: American Management Association, 1968.

59. Hain, Elwood B., Jr. "Black Labor in the Boston Construction Industry." Unpublished Master's thesis, Harvard Law School, 1969.

60. Hammond, Reese. "Effective Preparation for Apprenticeship," *Proceedings of the Twenty-Second Annual Meeting of the Industrial*

Relations Research Association (December 29–30, 1969), pp. 55–65.

61. Harris, Horace T. "An Experiment in Laboratory Technician Training." Unpublished Master's thesis, University of Wisconsin, Madison, Wisconsin, 1969.

62. Hodgson, James D., and Marshall H. Brenner. "Successful Experience: Training Hardcore Unemployed," *Harvard Business Review*, vol. 46, no. 5 (September–October, 1968), pp. 148–156.

63. Hopper, Kenneth. "The Growing Use of College Graduates as Foremen," *Management of Personnel Quarterly*, vol. 6, no. 2 (Summer, 1967), pp. 2–12.

64. Horowitz, Morris A., and Irwin L. Herrnstadt. *A Study of the Training of Tool and Die Makers*. Boston: Northeastern University, 1969.

65. Iacobelli, John L. "A Survey of Employer Attitudes Toward Training the Disadvantaged," *Monthly Labor Review*, vol. 93, no. 6 (June, 1970), pp. 51–55.

66. ———. "Training Programs of Private Industry in the Greater Cleveland Area." Unpublished Ph.D. thesis, Department of Economics, University of Texas, June, 1969.

67. "Industrial Investment in Manpower," *New England Business Review* (February, 1965), pp. 1–5.

68. Janger, Allen R., and Ruth G. Shaeffer. *Managing Programs to Employ the Disadvantaged*. Studies in Personnel Policy, No. 219. National Industrial Conference Board, 1970.

69. Johnson, David B., and James L. Stern. "Why and How Workers Shift from Blue-Collar to White-Collar Jobs," *Monthly Labor Review*, vol. 92, no. 10 (October, 1969), pp. 7–13.

70. Kaufman, Jacob J., *et al. The Role of the Secondary Schools in the Preparation of Youth for Employment—Summary, Conclusions, and Recommendations*. University Park, Pa.: Institute for Research on Human Resources, February, 1967.

71. Kincaid, Harry V., and Edward A. Podesta, "An Exploratory Survey of Proprietary Vocational Schools," *Research in Vocational and Technical Education*. Proceedings of a Conference, June 10–11, 1966. Center for Studies in Vocational and Technical Education, University of Wisconsin, Madison, Wisconsin, 1967, pp. 202–222.

72. Kleingartner, Archie. "The Characteristics and Work Adjustment of Engineering Technicians," *California Management Review*, vol. 11, no. 3 (Spring, 1969), pp. 89–96.

73. Levitan, Sar A., Garth L. Mangum, and Robert Taggart III. *Economic Opportunity in the Ghetto: The Partnership of Government and Business*. A Joint Publication of the Center for Manpower Studies,

George Washington University, and the National Manpower Policy Task Force. Baltimore: The Johns Hopkins Press, 1970.

74. Liebow, Elliott. *Tally's Corner: A Study of Street Corner Men.* Boston: Little, Brown & Co., 1967.

75. Likert, Rensis. *The Human Organization.* New York: McGraw-Hill Book Company, 1967.

76. ————. *New Patterns of Management.* New York: McGraw-Hill Book Company, 1960.

77. "Managers Go Back to School at Western Electric Training Center," *Administrative Management* (August, 1969), pp. 24–25.

78. *Manpower Report of the President.* March, 1970.

79. Marcson, Simon. "The Utilization of Scientific and Engineering Manpower in Industry," *California Management Review*, vol. 12, no. 4 (Summer, 1970), pp. 33–42.

80. Margulies, Newton, and Anthony P. Raia. "Scientists, Engineers and Technology Obsolescence." *California Management Review*, vol. 10, no. 2 (Winter, 1967), pp. 43–48.

81. Marks, Samuel B. "Employer Techniques for Upgrading Low-Skill Workers," *Proceedings of the Twenty-First Annual Winter Meeting of the Industrial Relations Research Association.* Chicago: December 29–30, 1968.

82. Marshall, F. Ray, and Vernon M. Briggs, Jr. *Equal Apprenticeship Opportunities: The Nature of the Issue and the New York Experience.* Policy Papers in Human Resources and Industrial Relations No. 10. Institute of Labor and Industrial Relations, The University of Michigan-Wayne State University. Ann Arbor: A Joint Publication with the National Manpower Policy Task Force, November, 1968.

83. ————. *The Negro and Apprenticeship.* Baltimore: The Johns Hopkins Press, 1967.

84. McGregor, Douglas. *The Human Side of Enterprise.* New York: McGraw-Hill Book Company, 1960.

85. McLennen, Kenneth. "Education and Training for Managerial Jobs," *American Journal of Economics and Sociology*, vol. 28, no. 4 (October, 1969), pp. 423–436.

86. McNamara, Walter J. "Retraining Industrial Personnel," *Personnel Psychology*, vol. 16, no. 3 (Autumn, 1963), pp. 233–247.

87. Mills, D. Quinn. *Industrial Relations and Manpower in Construction* Cambridge, Massachusetts: M.I.T. Press, forthcoming, 1972.

88. ————. "The Construction Industry: Adjustments to Minority Group Entry." Unpublished manuscript, January, 1970.

89. Mollenkopf, William G. "Some Results of Three Basic Skills Training

Programs in an Industrial Setting," *Journal of Applied Psychology,* vol. 55, no. 5 (1969), pp. 343–347.

90. Mooney, Joseph D. "An Analysis of Unemployment among Professional Engineers and Scientists," *Industrial and Labor Relations Review,* vol. 19, no. 4 (July, 1966), pp. 517–518.

91. Morse, Dean. *The Peripheral Worker.* New York: Columbia University Press, 1969.

92. Muir, Allen A., *et al.* "Cost-Effectiveness Analysis of On-the-Job and Institutional Training Courses." Washington, D.C.: Manpower Administration, U.S. Department of Labor, 1967. (Mimeographed.)

93. Myers, Charles A., and George P. Shultz. *The Dynamics of a Labor Market.* Englewood Cliffs, N.J.: Prentice-Hall, Inc., 1951.

94. Nadler, Leonard. "Helping the Hard-Core Adjust to the World of Work," *Harvard Business Review,* vol. 48, no. 2 (March–April, 1970), pp. 117–126.

95. National Alliance of Businessmen. "Outlook," *First Annual Report,* Circa 1969.

96. National Industrial Conference Board. *Education, Training, and Employment of the Disadvantaged.* Studies in Public Affairs, no. 4, 1969.

97. National Manpower Policy Task Force. *Improving the Nation's Manpower Programs.* Washington, D.C.: February, 1970.

98. Nemore, Arnold, and Garth L. Mangum. "Private Involvement in Federal Manpower Programs," in Arnold R. Weber *et al.* (eds.), *Public-Private Manpower Policies.* Industrial Relations Research Association Series, 1969.

99. Nevins, Raphael F., and Andrew Merryman. "The Search for Black Management," *The MBA,* vol. 3, no. 7 (April–May, 1969), pp. 8–14.

100. *New York Times,* January 28, 1970.

101. *New York Times,* February 11, 1970.

102. *New York Times,* April 19, 1970.

103. *New York Times,* June 21, 1970.

104. *New York Times,* July 10, 1970.

105. *New York Times,* July 20, 1970.

106. *New York Times,* July 31, 1970.

107. *New York Times,* September 7, 1970.

108. *New York Times,* December 5, 1970.

109. Norgren, Paul H. *Obsolescence and Updating of Engineers' and Scientists' Skills.* Report for the Office of Manpower Policy, U.S. Department of Labor, MDTA-1-64, November, 1966.

110. Northrup, Herbert R., *et al. Negro Employment in Basic Industry—A Study of Racial Policies in Six Industries,* vol. 1. Philadelphia:

Industrial Research Unit, Wharton School of Finance and Commerce, University of Pennsylvania, 1970.

111. Northrup, Herbert R. *The Negro in Aerospace Industry*. Philadelphia: University of Pennsylvania Press, 1968.

112. Orton, Eliot. "Work Experience as a Factor in the Entry Labor Market." Unpublished Ph.D. dissertation, Department of Economics, Cornell University, 1968.

113. Palmer, Gladys L. *Labor Mobility in Six Cities*. New York: Social Science Research Council, 1954.

114. Patten, Thomas H., Jr. "Organization Processes and the Development of Managers: Some Hypotheses," Human Organization, vol. 26, no. 4 (Winter, 1967), pp. 242–255.

115. Perlman, Richard. *On-the-Job Training in Milwaukee—Nature, Extent, and Relationship to Vocational Education*. Madison: University of Wisconsin, 1969.

116. Pigors, Paul, and Charles A. Myers. *Personnel Administration*, sixth edition. New York: McGraw-Hill Book Company, 1969. Chapter 20.

117. Piore, Michael J. "On-the-Job Training in the Dual Labor Market: Public and Private Responsibilities in On-the-Job Training of Disadvantaged Workers," in Weber *et al.* (eds.), *Public-Private Manpower Policies*. Industrial Relations Research Association Series, 1969.

118. *Private Industry and the Disadvantaged Worker*. Prepared for the Urban Coalition. New York and Washington, D.C.: E. F. Shelley and Company, Inc., January, 1969.

119. Puma, John J. "Improving Negro Employment in Boston," *Industrial Management Review*, vol. 8, no. 1 (Fall, 1966), pp. 37–45. Sloan School of Management, Massachusetts Institute of Technology.

120. Purcell, Theodore V., and Rosalind Webster. "Window on the Hardcore World," *Harvard Business Review*, vol. 47, no. 4 (July-August, 1969), pp. 118–129; also (30).

121. Raudsepp, Eugene. *Managing Creative Scientists and Engineers*. New York: The Macmillan Company, 1963.

122. "Remarks by William R. Bechtel," May 13, 1970, which followed the report of Senator Gaylord Nelson's Subcommittee, *The JOBS Program (Job Opportunities in the Business Sector) Background Information*. Washington, D.C.: U.S. Government Printing Office, May, 1970.

123. Reynolds, Lloyd G. *The Structure of Labor Markets*. New York: Harper and Row, 1951.

124. Rhine, Shirley H., and Daniel Creamer. *The Technical Manpower Shortage: How Acute?* New York: National Industrial Conference Board, 1969.

125. Rosen, Hjalmar, and Melvin Blonsky. "Dual Standards in Employing the Hard Core," *Personnel Administration* (March-April, 1970), pp. 4–7.

126. Rosen, R. A. Hudson. "The Hard Core and the Puritan Ethic," *Manpower*, vol. 1, no. 2 (January, 1970), p. 30.

127. Rosendorf, Sidney. "Data Firm Finds Answer in Ghetto," *Manpower*, vol. 1, no 2 (January, 1970), pp. 25–28.

128. Saltzman, Arthur W. "Manpower Planning in Private Industry," in Arnold R. Weber *et al.* (eds.), *Public-Private Manpower Policies* Madison, Wisconsin: Industrial Relations Research Association Series, 1969.

129. Schein, Edgar H. "Forces Which Undermine Management Development," California Management Review, vol. 5, no. 4 (Summer, 1963), pp. 23–24.

130. Schein, Edgar H., and Warren G. Bennis. *Personal and Organizational Change Through Group Methods: The Laboratory Approach.* New York: John Wiley and Sons, Inc., 1965.

131. Scoville, James G. *The Job Content of the U.S. Economy, 1940–70.* New York: McGraw-Hill Book Company, 1969.

132. Shlensky, Bertram C. "Determination of Turnover in JOBS Programs." Unpublished Ph.D. dissertation, Massachusetts Institute of Technology, September, 1970.

133. Shultz, George P., and Arnold R. Weber. *Strategies for the Displaced Worker.* New York: Harper & Row, 1966.

134. Slichter, Sumner H., James J. Healy, and E. Robert Livernash. *The Impact of Collective Bargaining on Management.* Washington, D.C.: The Brookings Institution, 1960.

135. Somers, Gerald G. "Pilot Feasibility Study of Training in Business and Industry." Unpublished study for the Office of Research and Development, Manpower Adminstration, U.S. Department of Labor. Washington, D.C., 1970.

136. Spain, James S. "A Modest Proposal for the Abatement of Corporate Racism," *The MBA*, vol. 4, no. 7 (April, 1970), pp. 16–20, 63–65.

137. Spain, James S., Clarence M. Sunnaville, Jr., William Pickens, III, and Kendall Nash. "Black Executives: The Darkie at the Bottom of the Stairs," *The MBA*, vol. 3, no. 7 (April-May, 1969), p. 41.

138. Steinmetz, Lawrence L. "Age: Unrecognized Enigma of Executive Development," *Management of Personnel Quarterly*, vol. 8, no. 3 (Fall, 1969), pp. 2–12.

139. Stewart, Rosemary. "Managers for Tomorrow," in *Problems of Progress in Industry*, H. M. Stationery Office, London, No. 2, 1957.

140. Strauss, George. "Apprentice-Related Instruction: Some Basic Issues,"

Journal of Human Resources, vol. 3, no. 2 (Spring, 1968), pp. 213–236.

141. ———. "Apprenticeship: An Evaluation of the Need," in Arthur M. Ross (ed.), *Employment Policy and the Labor Market*. Berkeley, California: University of California Press, 1965.

142. Streiner, Herbert E. "The Opportunities Industrialization Center: A Successful Demonstration of Minority Self-Help, Training and Education," in *The Education and Training of Racial Minorities*, Proceedings of a Conference, May 11–12, 1967, Center for Studies in Vocational and Technical Education, University of Wisconsin, Madison, Wisconsin.

143. Sullivan, Leon H. *Build Brother Build*. Philadelphia: Mcrea Smith Company, 1969.

144. "Summary of Major Findings, Conclusions and Recommendations on Job Opportunities in the Business Sector (JOBS) Program: Study by Greenleigh Associates, Inc.," *Daily Labor Report*, September 17, 1970.

145. Taylor, David P., and Michael J. Piore. "Federal Training Programs for Dispersed Employment Occupations." Department of Economics working paper, Massachusetts Institute of Technology, July 1969. (Mimeographed; to be published in a volume of essays, *Issues in Labor Policy*, by M.I.T. Press, Spring, 1971.)

146. *The Engineering Profession: A New Profile*. A report from the National Engineers Register, Engineers Joint Council. New York, 1969.

147. *The JOBS Program (Job Opportunities in the Business Section) Background Information*. A report by Senator Gaylord Nelson's Subcommittee. Washington, D.C.: U.S. Government Printing Office, May, 1970.

148. *The Transition from School to Work*. A report based on the Princeton Manpower Symposium, May 9–10, 1968, at Princeton University. Published by the Industrial Relations Section, 1969.

149. U.S. Department of Commerce. *Technical Manpower for the U.S. Economy*. Report of the Panel on Technical Manpower and its Importance for the U.S. Economy. Washington, D.C.: U.S. Government Printing Office, December, 1968.

150. U.S. Department of Labor, Manpower Administration. *Apprentice Training*. Washington, D.C.: U.S. Government Printing Office, 1969.

151. U.S. Department of Labor, Bureau of Apprenticeship and Training. *Career Patterns of Former Apprentices*. Washington, D.C.: U.S. Government Printing Office, 1959.

152. U.S. Department of Labor, *Formal Occupational Training of Adult*